ENJOY:
A SUPERNATURAL ECHO
A SPIRITUAL AWAKENING

THE TITLE WAS ANOTHER
WHISPER FROM WITHIN
MY HEART.

GOD'S VOICE!

A SUPERNATURAL ECHO/A SPIRITUAL AWAKENING

Interior design/Cover design: Lutricia Lopez
lutricialopez.youarefree@gmail.com

Editor: Rebecca Hallock
bhallock80@gmail.com

Published by:
Penny Plaster Beavers
Email: penny_plaster@yahoo.com

ISBN print: 9798871568071

Library of Congress Control Number: pending
Categories: Non-Fiction / Self-Help / Christian
Printed in the United States of America

The 365 Daily Devotional
to stir yourself up and build a
relationship with:
God
Jesus Christ
Holy Spirit

Make it personal.

You pick the day.

ONE

Ephesians 2:14

For he himself is our peace, who has made the two groups one and has destroyed the barrier, the dividing wall of hostility.

In Jesus name Amen

When you are talking with someone about God who is not born again, they are the Gentiles. They have a challenging time understanding you because there is a wall separating them. Get them to understand how very much God loves them and get them to do one step at a time. First, get them born again. Now the wall has been torn down because they belong to God. Jesus did the work! If they accept Jesus, the WALL is down. Now their spirit has been renewed. Be patient! With prayer and gentleness, you can help them see how important it is to live by God's Word in this world.

NEVER GIVE UP!!

TWO

Romans 15:13

May the God of hope fill you with all joy and peace in believing, so that by the power of the Holy Spirit you may abound in hope.

In Jesus name Amen

Hope in God is accepting His Word to work no matter your situation!!

Hope brings joy and peace to your heart. This is a wonderful place to be with God! The Holy Spirit's power is right there in your belief!!

THREE

1 Corinthians 13:4-8

Love is patient, love is kind. It does not envy, it does not boast, it is not proud. It is not rude, it is not self-seeking, it is not easily angered, it keeps no record of wrongs. Love does not delight in evil but rejoices with the truth. It always protects, always trusts, always hopes, always perseveres. Love never fails.

In Jesus name Amen

Be Bold for God and go and stand on Truth!!!!

FOUR

Jeremiah 33:3

Call me and I will answer you and tell you great
and hidden things you have not known.

In Jesus name Amen

If you are in the Kingdom of God, you are a
child of God which means you can ask
questions and get answers.

So, when you go to bed ask your question to
the Almighty God and King of Kings. Now, go to
sleep knowing He hears you and thank Him for
your answer in the morning regarding your
situation. Trust your God!

Yes, He truly is a wonderful, awesome God!!

God knew the answer before you had the problem, just ask Him, knowing He will answer!!

Life with God is the coolest way of life.

FIVE

2 Corinthians 2:17

For we are not, like so many, peddlers of God's word, but as men of sincerity, as commissioned by God, in the sight of God we speak in Christ.

In Jesus name Amen

Did you know you can make a demand on the Word of God? It is not a demand on God, it's a demand on His provision that He has already made for us!!

If it is in the Bible, that doesn't mean you get it, unless you make a demand on His Word. It's important that you don't doubt or cast the Word down while you wait! If you could have Jesus stand in front of you and hear what He is saying about your situation, you would walk away excited!

If I have money in the bank, I walk in and show my bank card and that's a demand on what is already mine. This is exactly how God's Word works! Get excited!! He is closer than right in front of you and His Spirit lives inside of you.

SIX

1 Peter 4:10-11

Each of you should use whatever gift you have received to serve others, as faithful stewards of God's grace in its various forms.
If anyone speaks, they should do so as one who speaks the very words of God. If anyone serves, they should do so with the strength God provides, so that in all things God may be praised through Jesus Christ. To him be the glory and the power for ever and ever.

In Jesus name Amen

Your gift, that God gave you is for me just as my gift that God gave me, is for you. As we do everything in love for each other, our spiritual man is growing toward God and His ways. This is so much better for us and it's allowing Jesus to shine through us. Without a doubt, we can give God all the Glory and praise, for showing us and guiding us in an unselfish life. Look unto God for this strength. Oh, what a beautiful feeling it is to serve others in "God's GRACE."

It will change your outlook and your heart.

SEVEN

Hebrews 4:16

Let us then with confidence draw near to the throne of grace, that we may receive mercy and find grace to help in time of need.

In Jesus name Amen

Go ahead and run to the throne room anytime, anyplace, any way you can!

God made it possible for YOU!

God is waiting just for YOU!

EIGHT

1 John 4:4

Little children, you are from God and have overcome them, for he who is in you is greater than he who is in the world.

In Jesus name Amen

You got this with the Lord!

Just remember to do it God's way, not your way!

When you do it God's way, YOU'VE GOT THIS because now you are letting God lead you and not your flesh or selfish ways!!

Stop and really understand that HE TRULY LIVES INSIDE YOU!

Make Him a proud Papa, who does honor you and loves YOU so much!!

YOU'VE GOT THIS WITH GOD, YOU OVERCOMER, YOU!

NINE

Proverbs 11:12

Whoever belittles his neighbor lacks sense, but a man of understanding remains silent.

In Jesus name Amen

Are you a person that lacks the sense of God?

Or

Are you a person with an understanding of God?

TEN

Romans 8:9

You, however, are not in the flesh but in the Spirit, if in fact the Spirit of God dwells in you. Anyone who does not have the Spirit of Christ does not belong to him.

In Jesus name Amen

God loves all the people in the world! But not all people are called His children. Do you want what God has for all His children? Come and be a part of this great family that will live forever. If you need to step up and jump off the lukewarm fence, today is a fine day to do it. Come to the Lord or come back home! You all are welcome!!

ELEVEN

1 Corinthians 16:14

Let all that you do be done in love.

In Jesus name Amen

Is it that simple?

Yes, it is! When you fall in love with Jesus, it is that easy to share that love in all that you do.

TWELVE

Ephesians 5:15-20

Look carefully at how you walk, not as unwise but as wise,
making the best use of the time, because the days are evil.
Therefore, do not be foolish but understand what the will of the Lord is.
And do not get drunk with wine, for that is debauchery, but be filled with the Spirit,
addressing one another in psalms and hymns and spiritual songs, singing and making melody to the Lord with your heart,
giving thanks always for all things to God the Father in the name of our Lord Jesus Christ.

In Jesus name Amen

Look into your heart and see if you are truly living in the Will of God before you bad mouth Christians around you. If you are spending time looking for bad in people who are called to do God's work, you're wasting your time, and you are unwise. Walking with God calls us to search our own hearts and for us to read His Word for ourselves to do the Will of the Lord. To bring someone down is not what God has called you to do. It is not a mind thing as the world thinks, It's a heart thing from the Spirit! If you are filled with the Spirit, you will show love. If you are around such people who do try to bring people down, pray for them and ask God to lead you in sharing His true Will from His Word to them. Sometimes after a while, you may even hear God say to you: "walk away." Just be obedient and know God will send someone else to help that person. Always keep them in prayer.

God never gives up on anyone!

God is Love.

THIRTEEN

John 1:12

But to all who did receive him, who believed in his name, he gave the right to become children of God.

In Jesus name Amen

Notice people around you and be a help to those who want to believe or already believe to grow in their faith. He has made a way for them and does give them the right to be His children. He did it for you as well. Not by your standard, but by His love and His son.

Be a help and not a hindrance.

You bring them to God and He will clean them.

FOURTEEN

1 Corinthians 1:27-28

But God chose the foolish things of the world to shame the wise; God chose the weak things of the world to shame the strong.
God chose the lowly things of this world and the despised things and the things that are not to nullify the things that are...

In Jesus name Amen

The leading of God seems foolish so people will not move on it. Most people will try to make it fit their wisdom of men or their religion. Therefore, you have delayed your blessing. Because to make it fit into man's wisdom will have absolutely no effect. You just killed God's calling in that situation. Don't conform God's ideas to man or this world. When God told the lady (who had just enough food for herself and her son) to feed someone else with what she had, sounded like a foolish thing to do. BUT GOD!! The lady obeyed and when she did as God had instructed her, she received her blessings.

When God tells you to give away what you need, it's not foolishness. It is more wisdom than your mind can handle.

If you have an ear to hear and will act on whatever God says to do, you have become a wise man.

To KNOW God is your Father who will take care of you, your trust grows, then your faith kicks in! No stopping you now in the name of Jesus Christ!

FIFTEEN

Psalm 49:3

My mouth shall speak wisdom; the meditation of my heart shall be understanding.

In Jesus Name Amen

When you spend time meditating on God's Word, the Holy Spirit will guide you.

Men read the Word as a story but can't understand the spiritual part.

You follow the teaching of the Holy Spirit!

Religion rejects it and will NEVER get it.

SIXTEEN

Ephesians 5:1-2

Therefore, be imitators of God, as beloved children.
And walk in love, as Christ loved us and gave himself up for us, a fragrant offering and sacrifice to God.

In Jesus name Amen

Imitators: "A person who copies the behavior or actions of another."

Are you allowed to be like God?

In His very own words, YES!

Go and be like your Father, make Him proud!
Make Him smile!

It's all about Him and His Love for you and the
world.

SEVENTEEN

James 5:15-16

And the prayer offered in faith will make the
sick person well; the Lord will raise them up. If
they have sinned, they will be forgiven.
Therefore confess your sins to each other and
pray for each other so that you may be healed.
The prayer of a righteous person is powerful
and effective.

In Jesus name Amen

Do we need each other?

Absolutely!

Does God's Word work?

Yes!

When we step out and act in faith and know WE are powerful and effective because of Jesus Christ, signs and wonders will follow.

Now hear the Holy Spirit that lives inside of you:

"LET ME OUT and let's do what you were called to do!"

EIGHTEEN

Luke 10:19

Behold, I have given you authority to tread on serpents and scorpions, and over all the power of the enemy, and nothing shall hurt you.

In Jesus name Amen

What are you doing with your authority and power in the Mighty Name of JESUS CHRIST?

It is not because you're "good" or "bad" that determines if you receive it or not. Born again people have ALL the POWER and AUTHORITY!!! What are you doing for God Almighty on this Earth? This is for here and now, not in Heaven. God loves His children and gives you this to go preach and tell everyone about the "Good News" of Jesus Christ!!

He has equipped you; you don't equip yourself. You only believe by faith and act on His Word.

He gave YOU this for signs and wonders to show how the God of Abraham, our God is alive and still the same yesterday, today, and forever!!

Go in confidence knowing what His Word says!!

NINETEEN

Romans 10:15

And how are they to preach unless they are sent? As it is written, "How beautiful are the feet of those who preach the good news!"

In Jesus name Amen

God sees you and every little smile that you give to someone, every little encouragement to others, every step you take to share God is sharing the "Good News."

Baby steps are great!

Keep stepping forward with God!

He loves you so much.

TWENTY

John 3:3

Jesus answered him, "Truly, truly, I say to you, unless one is born again, he cannot see the kingdom of God."

In Jesus name Amen

Be concerned with those around you. Do you ask them if they believe in Jesus Christ the son of God? Go a step further, one that is so important, and ask: "are you born again?"

Step out and help pull those who are in Hell, into Heaven. This is your first calling, "GO" step out and announce The Gospel, "The Good News" to ALL.

TWENTY-ONE

John 10:10

The thief comes only to steal and kill and destroy. I came that they may have life and have it abundantly.

In Jesus name Amen

The thief, who does not use force but does watch you, listens to you and when you are off guard, he comes and attacks. Stay on guard! Never get used to the things he sends by saying, "I guess this is going to be like this forever." Remember, he is listening to your words. That's how you open the door and when you look away, he walks in.

Life and death are in the words you speak. It all starts in the spiritual world and then it comes into the physical world.

You have more authority and power against Satan than you realize. Take your position in the spiritual world so you can control your future. God does lead you, but YOU'RE the one that decides to follow or not. Satan is quick and ready to kill, steal and destroy you with your very own words.

TWENTY-TWO

Mark 11:24-25

For this reason I am telling you, whatever things you ask for in prayer [in accordance with God's will], believe [with confident trust] that you have received them, and they will be given to you.
And when you stand praying, if you hold anything against anyone, forgive them, so that your Father in heaven may forgive you your sins.

In Jesus Name Amen

Why do we doubt the very Word of God?

Time to renew our minds. Time to give an ear to what God says, not what the world tells us, or that voice that laughs at you when you start to believe.

BE DIFFERENT!

Remember in grade school how they got us to learn the timetables? Man! Over and over again? Then we got it! We were meditating over and over and then we knew that we knew the whole thing!! No matter what, you knew that you knew it!!!

Meditate on the Word of God! Until you are saying it! Until you are living it! Until you believe it with all your heart!!!

No one can stop you with the Word backing you up!

It's not our faith in question, you don't have enough of God's Word in you to believe. Just keep meditating, it WILL come into your heart.

TWENTY-THREE

Psalm 100:1-5

A Psalm for giving thanks.

Make a joyful noise to the Lord, all the earth!
Serve the Lord with gladness! Come into his
presence with singing!
Know that the Lord, he is God! It is he who
made us, and we are his; we are his people, and
the sheep of his pasture.
Enter his gates with thanksgiving, and his
courts with praise! Give thanks to him; bless his
name!
For the Lord is good; his steadfast love endures
forever, and his faithfulness to all generations.

In Jesus name Amen

You have been silent long enough! If you're uncomfortable shouting to the Lord, do it in your car!!!

Shout your words unto the Lord!!

This is your "war cry" that you believe and trust in God, and this is your time to stand on the rock!

Satan will run because he will be confused when he sees you praise the Lord in whatever situation you're in when he wants you crying and worried.

This is your Victory CRY and Satan will run!!

Do it every day and watch your situation change in faster time than you realize.

SHOUT TO THE LORD with words of how great HE IS!!

TWENTY-FOUR

Luke 12:24

Consider the ravens: they neither sow nor reap, they have neither storehouse nor barn, and yet God feeds them. Of how much more value are you than the birds!

In Jesus name Amen

The birds must search and seek and find their food which God has already supplied for them. They can't just hang around on an electric line sleeping or sit in trees all day and sing. They have to do their part and God always supplies their needs.

You are so much more valuable than a raven. The two things the birds never do are: worry and fear! They weren't made to do that, and neither are YOU!!!

Do your part without the worry and fear weighing you down!

In ALL things, always do it God's way!

You will be fed! You will be clothed, and all your needs WILL be fulfilled!!!!!

TWENTY-FIVE

1 Peter 3:15

But in your hearts honor Christ the Lord as holy, always being prepared to make a defense to anyone who asks you for a reason for the hope that is in you; yet do it with gentleness and respect.

In Jesus name Amen

Always stand for what God has said and has given to us in writing.

Be gentle and respectful, but you will need to be bold. It is God you stay true to without bending His Words left or right! You can't have half solid ground and the other side sand; your house will go down!! It will be slow, but it will go down!!

Stay true to God and honor Him! Your house will stand!

It's not always easy, but it's not about "easy" or "hard", it's about trusting in the Lord no matter what you're facing.

TWENTY-SIX

2 Timothy 4:7

I have fought the good fight, I have finished the race, I have kept the faith.

In Jesus name Amen

The most important act is to keep your Faith in God growing and strong.

TWENTY-SEVEN

Proverbs 18:20-21

From the fruit of their mouth a person's stomach is filled; with the harvest of their lips, they are satisfied.
The tongue has the power of life and death, and those who love it will eat its fruit.

In Jesus name Amen

If you say nothing aloud, guess what you get, nothing worthwhile!

If you speak against what God is saying, you get what Satan has for you, nothing worthwhile!

If you speak aloud the Words of God, you get EVERYTHING WORTHWHILE!

TWENTY-EIGHT

Ephesians 5:4

Let there be no filthiness nor foolish talk nor crude joking, which are out of place, but instead let there be thanksgiving.

In Jesus name Amen

Be in order of God's Word.

He lives in you and hears you.

Love Him enough to follow His wisdom.

TWENTY-NINE

Ephesians 5:20

Giving thanks always and for everything to God the Father in the name of our Lord Jesus Christ.

In Jesus name Amen

If you never give thanks to our God the Father, today is the day!

If you always do, speak out your blessings and thank Him. He has time, do you? Morning or night, make time for the one who loves you so unconditionally and give thanks for EVERYTHING!!

THIRTY

Acts 16:23-25

When they had struck them with many blows, they threw them into prison, commanding the jailer to guard them securely;
and he, having received such a command, threw them into the inner prison and fastened their feet in the stocks.
But about midnight Paul and Silas were praying and singing hymns of praise to God, and the prisoners were listening to them.

In Jesus name Amen

They both were still praying and singing!! This is our victory! When things get rough, start your very own prayer and song right in the middle of your troubles. This is the way to get your victory right in front of your enemies!

Paul and Silas did, and this is a great lesson to learn and apply to our lives starting now!!

THIRTY-ONE

Mark 6:31

And he said to them, "Come away by yourselves to a desolate place and rest a while." For many were coming and going, and they had no leisure even to eat.

In Jesus name Amen

We can lay down our heavy load of this world, which likes to wrap us up in problems and in hurt and carry us far from God. Stop and rest! Yes, Spiritual rest but don't forget physical rest is much needed and just as important. Take time this week to rest, take a nap and during this time, draw close to God. He wants to hold you during this time, please let Him.

God knows all and He is taking care of things while we rest in His arms in faith that it will be ok. Because in Jesus Christ, it WILL be more than ok!!

THIRTY-TWO

1 Peter 1:17

And if you call on him as Father who judges impartially according to each one's deeds, conduct yourselves with fear throughout the time of your exile.

In Jesus name Amen

If you are born again and call on the Father as your God and don't tithe, witness, or do anything for the Kingdom of God, your rewards are different from those who do tithe, who do witness, and give to the poor. Jesus died for your sins, your sins have been forgiven and they are not judged. His blood did that for US! Now your deeds that you do WILL be rewarded or judged. Do you get rewards? Don't stand in front of your God whom you call Father with no rewards to be handed to you. God is a just God. Read it again. This is fact and truth.

Do not FEAR; Be in awe of the GREAT Jehovah!

THIRTY-THREE

James 3:14-16

But if you have bitter jealousy and selfish ambition in your hearts, do not boast and be false to the truth.
This is not the wisdom that comes down from above, but is earthly, unspiritual, demonic.
For where jealousy and selfish ambition exist, there will be disorder and every vile practice.

In Jesus name Amen

Wow! Don't take the pill of jealousy or selfishness.

Flush them both!

This will cause disorder big time!

They will take you down faster than you realize!

THIRTY-FOUR

Romans 10:17

So, faith comes from hearing, and hearing through the word of Christ.

In Jesus name Amen

You can put your faith in a lot of people and even have faith in yourself, but it is a road with a dead end. True faith that lasts and the faith that changes your life is hearing the Word that comes from God!

You cannot hear it once and say I got this! God says faith comes from hearing and hearing His Word!

Faith in God is an open road!

You must keep hearing His word to build your faith.

Enjoy your choice.

THIRTY-FIVE

Matthew 24:10-12

And then many will fall away and betray one another and hate one another.
And many false prophets will arise and lead many astray.
And because lawlessness will be increased, the love of many will grow cold.

In Jesus name Amen

It will happen! Don't be one of those that fall away. Hate will start instead of forgiveness, and you just try to justify it by the way you're feeling, and this is not of God!

False prophets are clever. Always check what is being said to you against the Word of the Lord. He said many WILL be led away.

Guard your heart with the Word of the Lord. Keep it in your heart and on your lips. Don't give up an inch of what is right to do a little wrong. All Satan needs is just one little inch to try to take control over your life. Don't fall asleep on your watch or let your guard down. Always be watchful and diligent. No FEAR, just use Wisdom from the BIBLE.

THIRTY-SIX

Luke 7:22

So, he replied to the messengers, "Go back and report to John what you have seen and heard: The blind receive sight, the lame walk, those who have leprosy are cleansed, the deaf hear, the dead are raised, and the good news is proclaimed to the poor."

In Jesus name Amen

If you have a testimony of things the Lord Jesus Christ has done for you, why do you hide that light? The testimony is not about you but what the Lord Jesus Christ has done and what He will do for others. If you don't share, how will others know He is alive today and still the same yesterday, today, and always?

Satan will tell you when you share your testimony that you're bragging about yourself and that you are puffed up and full of pride. Satan only speaks lies. If you share what the

Lord Jesus Christ has done in your life, Satan knows it will draw others to the Lord and he wants them for himself to burn in Hell and to torture for infinity. Share the GOOD NEWS with the poor. The poor doesn't mean "no money," it means poor in spirit and/or poor in knowledge and truth of who the Lord Jesus Christ is and how deep that love goes!

Ask God to make a divine appointment for you and it will happen. A chance to help someone and show how much God loves them.

Share that testimony!!! It is not to hide under a bushel, oh no!!!!!

Shine! Shine! Shine!

THIRTY-SEVEN

Luke 8:21

But he answered them, "My mother and my brothers are those who hear the word of God and do it."

In Jesus name Amen

Do what He says, not what you have justified in your head to do and still do things your way. Yes, He knows your heart, but do you know what He says?

Two completely different things.

It's time to chew on the meat of the Word and get off the milk.

THIRTY-EIGHT

1 Peter 5:6

Humble yourselves, therefore, under the mighty hand of God so that at the proper time he may exalt you.

In Jesus name Amen

Don't let Satan put fear in you when God is now exalting you to a higher place where He needs you. Keep faith in Him because He knows the plans He has for you! They are plans to prosper you and not to hurt you. His ways are always MORE than great.

Hallelujah! Hallelujah! Hallelujah!

THIRTY-NINE

Jeremiah 7:23

But this command I gave them: 'Obey my voice, and I will be your God, and you shall be my people. And walk in all the way that I command you, that it may be well with you.

In Jesus name Amen

Read, believe, trust, and with faith, walk and apply His ways in your life. It will all be alright.

FORTY

1 Peter 2:16

Live as people who are free, not using your freedom as a cover-up for evil, but living as servants of God.

In Jesus name Amen

For the Lord in Heaven knows your heart.

Let the way you live honor your God who lives in Heaven.

FORTY-ONE

Proverbs 3:24

If you lie down, you will not be afraid; when you lie down, your sleep will be sweet.

In Jesus name Amen

God does not sleep. He gives you rest and sweet sleep. Lay down with His Words in your mouth and if you awake, just put His words in your mouth again. I sing in my Holy Language and back to sleep I go again!!!!

Your sleep WILL BE SWEET!

Kick your fear out the window and your sweet dreams will come!

FORTY-TWO

Romans 8:8

Those who are in the flesh cannot please God.

In Jesus name Amen

Don't allow your human side to override your Spiritual side!!

FORTY-THREE

1 Samuel 12:16

Now therefore stand still and see this great thing that the Lord will do before your eyes.

In Jesus name Amen

Keep your eyes on the Lord always!

Trust Him!

Have faith in Him.

Follow His ways!

REST!

FORTY-FOUR

2 Corinthians 10:5

We destroy arguments and every lofty opinion raised against the knowledge of God and take every thought captive to obey Christ.

In Jesus name Amen

Your mind is a place that starts a birth. Whatever you spend your time thinking about, is what you will give birth to. God says take every thought captive that is against the knowledge of Him.

What negative or positive things have you given birth to in your life?

Today is a new day to start paying attention to what you think. Cast anything down that is not from God and give birth to a new future. Not sure how to start? Find out what God says about you, and you say the same thing.

Tag you're it!

FORTY-FIVE

1 Peter 3:8

Finally, all of you, have unity of mind, sympathy, brotherly love, a tender heart, and a humble mind.

In Jesus name Amen

Keep this in your heart and put this in your mind for always!!!

FORTY-SIX

Ecclesiastes 7:8

Better is the end of a thing than its beginning, and the patient in spirit is better than the proud in spirit.

In Jesus name Amen

Some may begin with God but walk away before the end.

Some may not start out with God but end with God! That's when the end is better than the beginning.

FORTY-SEVEN

Proverbs 16:3

Commit your work to the Lord, and your plans will be established.

In Jesus name Amen

No matter who your boss is or how they treat you, always work like God in Heaven is your true boss!! Because He is the one to touch your boss's heart to bless you. Trust God and put your faith in Jesus Christ and relax. If it is time to change jobs, you will know deep in your heart. Talk with God and listen. He will establish your steps.

FORTY-EIGHT

1 John 3:17

But if anyone has the world's goods and sees his brother in need, yet closes his heart against him, how does God's love abide in him? Little children, let us not love in word or talk but indeed and in truth.

In Jesus name Amen

Your brother in Christ is your concern in the eyes of the Lord.

Don't turn your eyes away when you see a need and you can meet it. If you turn away, you are allowing man's way and Satan's way to dictate to you.

Always choose to follow God's way!!

FORTY-NINE

Hebrews 11:6

And without faith it is impossible to please him, for whoever would draw near to God must believe that he exists and that he rewards those who seek him.

In Jesus name Amen

Time to really get to know who God is. You need to realize He is a good God and not a genie in a bottle. You need to realize He is not out to get you.

Jesus came to take back what Adam GAVE to Satan. Adam gave away his/our authority and power to subdue this world. (Bring into control.) Not people, but your life and the situation around you. To take back your health by His stripes! Jesus Christ did so much before the cross to show you He is all about healing! Jesus did so much to teach us true love. Jesus went to Hell and took everything back that Adam gave away. It's truly yours! Now Jesus said it is finished and sat down by our Father. A relationship that is a two-way street. He did all the work, and we get all the benefits. Our part is to BELIEVE in Him and know what He has done for us is real. FAITH that moves you into saying everything He says. Doing things His way. You must change your thoughts and go before God and pray. Believe, keep your faith, and move on His Word. Start a new life and watch things change for you. Satan is fearful that you will find the truth. He knows it will set you free from him! Freedom is just a step away with the Words from God and the words you speak and act on. Another is to give what you worship - your money. It's God's way to see your true heart. Give to God and He always gives back and more. Satan is watching your words and watching your actions to see if you really believe and put faith in Jesus Christ. If you do, he knows he must bend his knee because you now know who you are in Jesus Christ and you really know you have authority over him. It's all about Jesus Christ and His way to bless you.

Be BLESSED!

FIFTY

Isaiah 41:13

For I, the Lord your God, hold your right hand; it is I who says to you, "Fear not, I am the one who helps you."

In Jesus name Amen

God is the same yesterday, today, and forever! God said fear NOT! Fear will leave you when you submit to do things God's way and resist the enemy.

Read it again. Who is the one who WILL help you? The God Most High! The one who will never leave you. Get rid of your fears by trusting what God tells you. Keep reading His Words. They are life and death in your life.

"I am the one who helps you." Praise God throughout your day and know today is the day that He has made, and Jesus Christ is the ONE who will help YOU.

FIFTY-ONE

Romans 12:21

Do not be overcome by evil but overcome evil with good.

In Jesus name Amen

Yes, this verse fights against our flesh. But when does our flesh ever win with a blessing? NEVER.

When the Word of God is followed, there is a big-time blessing!! YES!! Always!!

Go ahead and be wise, let your pride hurt and follow the Word of God. God will honor you and oh what blessings will be headed your way!!!

If you step out and do good when someone is doing evil, you could win their hearts for the Lord!!!

Oh, what a blessing!!!!!

FIFTY-TWO

1 Samuel 16:7

But the Lord said to Samuel, "Do not consider his appearance or his height, for I have rejected him. The Lord does not look at the things people look at. People look at the outward appearance, but the Lord looks at the heart."

In Jesus name Amen

That's what love does!

Thank You, Lord!!!

May we learn from you, Lord!!!

FIFTY-THREE

Psalm 25:5

Guide me in your truth and teach me, for you are God my Savior, and my hope is in you all day long.

In Jesus name Amen!!

Who do you have your hope in?

The most important is putting ALL YOUR HOPE in the Lord.

Your hope in the Lord is the flame in your heart. Keep your flame burning for God. All day long, every day!!

The world gives you false hope.

God gives love, guides you and teaches you what is true.

Real hope gives life!!

FIFTY-FOUR

Psalm 130:5

I wait for the Lord, my whole being waits, and in His Word, I put my hope.

In Jesus name Amen

When your hope is in the Word, you feel up-lifted! You feel complete, you say the Word out loud against what the world says. You stand strong!!!

Remember don't look at the situation, look at Jesus and what He says!!!

When things seem down, (at times they will) always go to God's Word and see what He says about things!!!

It may feel like an uphill battle, but our Lord is always working, even when you don't see it!!

Have hope and faith in the Lord and wait. While you're waiting...put on your praise!!!

God knows what He is doing.

Rest, kick your feet up and keep your Bible open.

FIFTY-FIVE

Romans 15:13

May the God of HOPE fill you with all joy and peace as you TRUST in him, so that you may overflow with HOPE by the power of the Holy Spirit.

In Jesus name Amen

As you stay TRUSTING your LORD, He gives you joy and peace! If your God is full of hope for you, then Hold On!! He made the earth, the sun, the moon, and He must know something to have HOPE in you! When you stop trusting the Lord, you have given up your power from God that has been given to you, The Holy Ghost!!

Never Give Up Hope!

God hasn't given up and He will never give up on you!

He has HOPE IN YOU!!

He knows the future, and it's a bright one!!

So, smile! Give Him the glory and know He sees and knows ALL for you!

FIFTY-SIX

Matthew 11:28

Come to me, all who labor and are heavy laden, and I will give you rest. Take my yoke upon you, and learn from me, for I am gentle and lowly in heart, and you will find rest for your souls. For my yoke is easy, and my burden is light.

In Jesus name Amen

Rest doesn't mean closing your Bible. It means letting go of worry and stress and reading and studying your Bible. Your confidence will grow, and then you will know when you rest, you are allowing God to move. You take on His Yoke. It's light because God moves on your behalf when you REST in HIM.

FIFTY-SEVEN

1 Timothy 6:12

Fight the good fight of FAITH, lay hold on eternal life, whereunto thou art also called, and hast professed a good profession before many witnesses.

In Jesus name Amen

Make sure your fight is to hold onto God's Word which builds you up and keeps you strong!! Fight the good fight of FAITH. The rest we are to resist, rebuke and stand strong!!

Resist... stand. (There is no fighting.)

Rebuke... finger waving. (No fight here! I love this one.)

When things happen that are not of God, STAND and wave your fingers in Satan's face. You CAN'T touch this, Satan!! (You MUST know this.)

Our fight has already been fought by Jesus and then Jesus sat down beside God. Your fight is to keep your FAITH, DO NOT let yourself get weak, this is dangerous!

Satan has lost and we have the VICTORY!!

We can always go deeper into the Word no matter how long you have been in the Word.

REPEAT what God has said out loud!!

Then rest in the Lord!!

FIFTY-EIGHT

James 2:14-17

What good is it, my brothers, if someone says he has faith but does not have works? Can that faith save him? If a brother or sister is poorly clothed and lacking daily food and one of you says to them, "Go in peace, be warmed and filled," Without giving them the things needed for the body, what good is that? So also, faith by itself if it does not have works, is dead.

In Jesus name Amen

Have compassion for others and always be ready to help feed and clothe when someone is in need. Faith and works go together. Have faith that if you give, God will always give back to you.

God says: "don't let your left hand see what your right hand is doing."

God sees all!!

Give and it will be given to you.

Our love for each other will keep us all helping each other!

FIFTY-NINE

Exodus 20:12

Honor your father and your mother, that your days may be long in the land that the Lord your God is giving you.

In Jesus name Amen

In your heart, love and honor your parents. You can honor them in distance if needed. Hold your parents up to the Lord in prayer every day. This is honor and a powerful love. A true sentiment from your heart.

SIXTY

Psalm 91:14-16

If you hold on to me for dear life," says God,
"I'll get you out of trouble. I'll give you the best
care if you'll only get to know and trust me.
Call me and I'll answer, be at your side in bad
time; I'll rescue you, then throw you a party.
(Honor you.)
I'll give you long life, give you a long drink of
salvation.

In Jesus name Amen

That's it!

SIXTY-ONE

2 Corinthians 4:18

So, we fix our eyes not on what is seen, but on what is unseen, since what is seen is temporary, but what is unseen is eternal.

In Jesus name Amen

The power of God is unseen at first, then it manifests in your world.

So, the Word says:

FIX your eyes on the unseen, it's more real than what you can see.

FIX your eyes on Jesus.

FIX your faith on Jesus, NOT MAN.

Keep your eyes on Jesus, not on the storm.

SIXTY-TWO

Proverbs 3:1-8

My child, never forget the things I have taught you. Store my commands in your heart.
If you do this, you will love many years, and your life will be satisfying.
Never let loyalty and kindness leave you! Tie them around your neck as a reminder. Write them deep within your heart.
Then you will find favor with both God and people, and you will earn a good reputation.
Trust in the LORD with all your heart; do not depend on your own understanding.
Seek his will in all you do, and he will show you which path to take.
Don't be impressed with your own wisdom.
Instead, fear the LORD and turn away from evil.
Then you will have healing for your body and strength for your bones.

In Jesus name Amen

SIXTY-THREE

John 10:18

No man taketh from me, but I lay it down of myself. I have power to lay it down, and I have power to take it again. This commandment have I received from my Father.

In Jesus name Amen

Jesus was given a COMMAND from God!

How much does He love you? God gave Jesus a command. (Order, instruction and direction.)

Do you realize Jesus could have walked away from all this pain, all this suffering? He knew what was ahead of Him!

Personally, I would say I would give my life for a friend. But the closer it would get to my suffering; I would be weighing things out. Hmmm, this person doesn't love me that much, why should I? This person is not worthy of my suffering one little bit. I would walk away and say NO!

Do you understand that before you gave your heart to Him, He already decided you were worth it?! He decided He loved you so much, He would do anything to save you from eternal death!! He knew we would be partying; He knew we would be ugly to people; He knew we would drink every weekend and pass out!

He did not have to take that beating, He didn't have to take all that suffering. But HE DID, so we, the guilty ones could walk away from this eternal death!!

Oh, what LOVE!!! Oh, what Praise we should have in our mouths before we get out of bed!!

Can you TRUST Jesus?

Yep!! This is who I want to have my back, this is who I want to go to court with if I need to go, this is who I want to move into my house to be my provider, this is who I want to take me in His arms and rest!

IN ALL SITUATIONS, I TRUST YOU, LORD JESUS!! THANK YOU, MY LORD!!

I will lift my hands!

I will sing out loud!

I will dance before you!

It's ALL about you, Lord!!

SIXTY-FOUR

John 10:11-12

I am the good shepherd. The good shepherd lays down his life for the sheep. The hired hand is not the shepherd and does not own the sheep. So, when he sees the wolf coming, he abandons the sheep and runs away. Then the wolf attacks the flock and scatters it.

In Jesus name Amen

Who do you want to be there for you?

The one who would die to save YOUR life, right?

So, relax and know you can trust Him!! Always!!

He loves your kids, He loves your parents, He loves your brother, He loves your sister, He loves your wife, He loves your husband, all before He gave them to you, He gave His life for them also. He is also their Good Shepherd!

When things seem to go crazy in your life and not the way you want them to, know your Shepherd has not left you and will never leave you! And He will never leave your loved ones!!

Keep your eyes on JESUS!!!

SIXTY-FIVE

Psalm 32:7

For you are my hiding place; you protect me from trouble. You surround me with songs of victory.

In Jesus name Amen

God gave me a vision...of a zipper.

When the zipper on a coat is down, you are not fully protected. When you use the zipper the way it was meant to be used, it pulls the two sides together, now you are protected!!

I saw us on one side of the zipper and God on the other side of the zipper. When we don't pull up on the zipper, we have space, empty space between us and we are not fully protected by His words. As we pull up on the zipper we draw nearer to God and His word daily. He comes nearer to us!!

With God's Word, we are pulled together.

We are fully protected!!

Don't forget to zip up with God today.

SIXTY-SIX

1 Corinthians 13:4-7

Love is patient, love is kind. It does not envy, it does not boast, it is not proud.
It does not dishonor others, It is not self-seeking, It is not easily angered, It keeps no record of wrongs.
Love does not delight in evil but rejoices with the truth.
It always protects, always trusts, always hopes, always perseveres.

In Jesus name Amen

Patient

Kind

No Envy

No Boasting

No Pride

No Dishonor

Not Self-seeking

Not Quick to Anger

No Record Keeping

Rejoices in Truth

Protects

Trusts

Hopes

Perseveres

Let's work on changing ourselves. One step at a time, one day at a time.

This is our LOVE walk.

We will always have an opportunity to show love.

Show people Love.

GOD is LOVE.

As you hear the Word of God and it goes into your heart, let the LOVE of God flow out of your heart toward others.

SIXTY-SEVEN

Psalm 107:2

Let the redeemed say so! Let those who have been redeemed by the LORD declare it – those whom he redeemed from the power of the enemy.

In Jesus name Amen

Redeemed: Retrieve, regain, get back, reclaim, repossess; buy back

Jesus has redeemed us!!

Jesus bought us back with His blood.

What did Jesus buy us back from?

Being a child of Satan!

We are no longer under his control, no longer living under his rules!! No longer under his power.

We have been adopted. We have a new Father!!!

So, PEOPLE say SO!!

You are free!!!

Study your new standard of life!!

You will find it in the Bible.

God's house is so big, He wants to adopt everyone!!

Let's say so and tell people the good news!!

SIXTY-EIGHT

Ephesians 1:7

In Him we have redemption through His blood, the forgiveness of our trespasses, according to the riches of His grace.

In Jesus name Amen

My last name is not SIN!

I have been adopted by the blood of Jesus!!

My last name is Redeemed!

Do you understand? God sees a child does not sin, they make mistakes.

Ask forgiveness for your mistake and walk the same as that day He adopted you!!! (When you got born again.)

A new way to look at things. From that day Jesus was on that cross and GAVE HIS life as a new testimony we walk in!

Shake off your past!

Shake off your chains!!

YOU ARE FREE FROM SIN!!

God picks you up every time you fail. If you sin, God could not look at you!!

You, my dear, are white as snow to God!!

Jesus did so much more than we understand. But the veil is torn, and we are to see Him in truth.

Put on your seatbelt, God's Word has much more to reveal to you as you grow in Him.

His word is The Living Word! FULLY ALIVE!!

Have you read God's Word? Give them spiritual eyes to see. Open their hearts! We have new things to learn, and God will guide us!!

Bite one word at a time and chew (study) on His Word.

Religion will tell you how bad you are! Religion will tell you; that you are not worthy!

Hey! Yes, you are good! Yes, you are worthy by the blood of Jesus!!!

Don't tell Jesus He is a liar!! That's Satan's job!!

Jesus did it all for us!!!

Walk redeemed!! Share the good news!!!

SIXTY-NINE

2 Corinthians 5:17

Therefore, if any man be in Christ, he is a new creature: old things are passed away; behold, all things are become new.

In Jesus name Amen

It's that easy!!!

Believe, study, and walk as the new man!!!

Your nature is new!!

The nature of God!!

Wanting what God wants.

SEVENTY

Psalms 78:24-25

He rained down manna upon them to eat and gave them food from heaven.
Man did eat the bread of angels; he sent them food in abundance.

In Jesus name Amen

Does OUR God still provide for us each day?

YES!

SEVENTY-ONE

Matthew 6:33

But seek ye first the kingdom of God and His righteousness, and all these things shall be added unto you.

In Jesus name Amen

We believe God for today and God will give us things we need tomorrow. Stress, worry, fear and anxiety are a gift from Satan I choose NOT to accept!!!!

I seek God and I accept His gift of His Word and His promises along with God's love for me. This gift He gives every day! I receive His gift. Every day He takes care of us.
Don't exchange His gift for Satan's.

As my Pastor said: "stop drop and roll." I am using it a little differently.
Stop - don't listen to Satan!!!
Drop - your fear, anxiety and stress onto God.
Roll - with God's gift!!

Tomorrow is God's to take care of.
Abundance: an exceptionally large quantity.
Our God is a big God!!!

SEVENTY-TWO

John 15:17

These things I command you, that ye love one another.

In Jesus name Amen

A true parent will ask and teach and command us to do different things in our growing up. The spirit world is the same as we grow, Our Heavenly Father is our Daddy who loves us so much. We may not understand all that He is doing and guiding us to do, but one day we will! Let's trust, and believe and have Faith in all things God tells, commands us and teaches us.

Keep walking, God is always holding your hand.

Treasure this from the Lord.

Command: order, tell, direct, instruct, call on and/or require.

Let's put the Lord's command into action in our life.

He is yours and you are His!!! Let's love each

other. In love, we will do anything to help each other! God's love is the best love to walk in.

We can do it, because when He commands, He already knows we CAN!!

SEVENTY-THREE

1 John 1:5-7

This is the message we have heard from him and declare to you: God is light; in him there is no darkness at all.
If we claim to have fellowship with him and yet walk in the darkness, we lie and do not live out the truth.
But if we walk in the light, as he is in the light, we have fellowship with one another, and the blood of Jesus, His Son, purifies us from all sin.

In Jesus name Amen

If you're a born-again Christian, you have God's nature inside you. Your nature is to search the Word of God to get to know Him. You come together in love with others to hear His Word. You really desire to do good. If you make a mistake, just ask God to forgive you and move on.

Jesus has delivered you!

Jesus has your burden!

Jesus has cleansed you!

Time to move on!!! Time to move forward!!

Satan has NO stronghold on you, the strings have been cut!!

God calls you strong and you are STRONG!!!

You are a new creature, follow your heart. Listen to that small voice that tells you truth.

Trust and believe God. Remember we have the situation; the situation DOES NOT have us!!

SEVENTY-FOUR

Matthew 27:46

At about three o'clock, Jesus called out with a loud voice, "El, Eli, lema sabachthani?" which means "My God, My God, why have you forsaken me?"

In Jesus name Amen

God could not look on Jesus when He took our sins!! Jesus said, why have you forsaken me? God knew when Jesus took our sins, He could not look at sin and turn away from Jesus and Jesus felt it. But Jesus was the only one who could take all our sin. He had no sin; He made the choice to TAKE it ALL from us!!

Satan could not accuse Jesus of anything!

And today Satan cannot accuse us unless we let him. When Jesus TOOK your sin, He gave you RIGHTEOUSNESS and MERCY. It's time to look at yourself the way God sees you. He does not turn away from you because Jesus took your sin and now, He can look upon you. He loves you and sees the best. You are righteous because of Jesus. It's a free gift! Receive this gift and be free today!!

My heart has this big explosion inside!!!

I AM FREE!!

I AM FREE!!

I AM FREE!!

SEVENTY-FIVE

1 John 2:14

I write to you, dear children
Because you know the Father.
I write to you, fathers,
Because you know him who is from the
beginning.
I write to you, young men,
Because you are strong,
And the word of God lives in you,
And you have overcome the evil one.

In Jesus name Amen

It's great to get an answer before the problem!!!

It's just like our Lord!!

It's great being born again!!

We are strong, says the Lord!!

The Holy One lives in us, says the Lord!!

We HAVE overcome the evil one! Says the
Lord!!

We just need to believe the Lord!!

We got it all!!!

SEVENTY-SIX

Act 3:16

By faith in the name of Jesus, this man whom you see and know was made strong. It is Jesus' name and the faith that comes through him that has completely healed him, as you can all see.

In Jesus name Amen

My testimony on seeing a miracle from my Lord, Jesus!!

My family lived on a farm. Mom and dad had four sons and one daughter (me). You really must understand, on the farm if animals were born deformed, they were killed. (Sorry, but this is a hard fact.) My dad had a heart of gold, but he was a farmer. We had a dog that had puppies. The runt of the puppies seemed different. As the puppies grew, we noticed that the runt was using only his front legs and dragging his back legs. Dad told us if he didn't get better, he would have to take care of it. We knew what that meant. That night five little kids prayed and cried out with all their hearts for that little puppy's healing. Our hearts were crying out for God to make his back legs work. We knew God's word enough to BELIEVE that by our faith, He heard us and would do it!! (Our grandmother taught us this.) We awaken the next morning with the puppies barking and wanting to go outside. We all came downstairs to see Dad looking at that runt who was standing on all four legs that were working as well as the other puppies' legs. Dad said, this is a miracle!! We told him, we all prayed and asked God to heal the puppy so he would live.

I still cry to this day when I tell this story. The story of a miracle for a puppy, for five kids and their dad to see it happen!

Now when I tell this story I hear God say, I will do way more for my children.

You may see me lay hands on someone and call on God and believe that He not only hears my prayers, but he answers them!

NO DOUBT AT ALL!! ALL GLORY, ALL GLORY TO MY LORD, MY HEALER!

Jehovah Rapha - The Lord Your Healer!

Sometimes I ask children who believe to pray for me, their little hearts are full of big faith.

SEVENTY-SEVEN

Matthew 18:15

If your brother sins against you, go and tell him his fault, between you and him alone. If he listens to you, you have gained your brother.

In Jesus name Amen

Let's talk things out.

Let's NOT tell everyone what someone has done to us.

Let's walk with the nature of Jesus, the new creation that we are.

We may get upset with each other at times, and that's ok. It's how we work things out between each other.

How great to fix a problem by talking? There are many steps when the person will not talk things out. But you, as a born-again child can take that first step.

Talk with love, and listen and share.

SEVENTY-EIGHT

John 1:14

The Word became flesh and made his dwelling among us. We have seen his glory, the glory of the one and only Son, who came from the Father, full of grace and truth.

In Jesus name Amen

God, Jesus, Holy Spirit, Grace, Love, Forgiveness!

What great gifts we have been given freely! We are so blessed!!

Waking up with a full heart of these gifts is a wonderful way to start your day Precious Children of God!!

Great PRAISE to our Lord and King!!

SEVENTY-NINE

Ephesians 4:26-27

In your anger do not sin" [a]: Do not let the sun go down while you are still angry and do not give the devil a foothold.

In Jesus name Amen

God gives us choices!

God feeds us wisdom.

Don't let your pride give the devil a foothold!!

Our flesh does not like God's way.

You can be angry but be careful with your words. Before the sun goes down take care of today's issues. Bring joy back in with forgiveness and kind words!

Why? Because God knows what is best for his children.

His way is the best way!!

God's way is wisdom in your life here and now!!

EIGHTY

2 Timothy 1:7

For God has not given us a spirit of fear and timidity, but of power, love, and self-discipline.

In Jesus name Amen

You have two lions in front of you. One looks powerful, he turns his head when he roars at you, he runs towards you and stops, nose to nose with you. He is making fear arise in your heart, but you see he has no teeth, he has no claws!!

The other lion is bigger and stronger. You can see the strength as he walks toward you, he has a powerful roar. He looks straight at you; you see his teeth and his feet are bigger and looks much stronger than the other lion. This lion has a calmness in his eyes.

For some reason, you feel no fear. You actually have a feeling of strong respect. As He walks closer and closer, your heart races! He walks past you; He turns and sits behind you. Your fear of the other lion is gone!!

Now you feel the power of this lion as He sits behind you. You feel His love for you. You are safe! You know when the other lion looks at you, he sees The LION OF JUDAH!!

FEAR NOT!!!

The weaker lion walks away. As he turns to leave, he looks at you and you hear him say "I will return." The LION OF JUDAH says, "I AM WITH YOU ALWAYS, FEAR NOT CHILD OF MINE!!"

(A vision I saw, and I wanted to share)

EIGHTY-ONE

1 John 5:4

For everyone born of God overcomes the world. This is the victory that has overcome the world, even our faith.

In Jesus name Amen

YOUR JOB IS TO USE YOUR FAITH!!

Know that YOUR faith in Jesus Christ secured YOUR victory in overcoming the world. In all situations.

Don't waver, don't doubt, stand your ground!!

Satan is powerful and clever, yes, but who can be against us, if God is for us?!

WE HAVE THE HOLY SPIRIT in us!! Every step!!

Stay in the Word and look for the verse that will build your faith in your situation.

YOU have the victory because of Jesus!!

Fight the good fight of faith!!!

EIGHTY-TWO

1 Samuel 17:45-47

David and Goliath

David said to the Philistine, "You come against me with sword and spear and javelin, but I come against you in the name of the Lord Almighty, the God of the armies of Israel, whom you have defied. This day the Lord will deliver you into my hands, and I'll strike you down and cut off your head. This very day I will give the carcasses of the Philistine army to the birds and the wild animal, and the whole world will know that there is a God in Israel. All those gathered here will know that is is not by sword or spear that the Lord saves; for the battle is the Lord's, and He will give all of you into our hands."

In Jesus name Amen

David knew his God!!

David's God is our very own God today! Any giant in your life that speaks against Our God is Satan, the great deceiver!

The giant called him names and laughed at David. The giant spoke words of death to David and made fun of His God. What did David do? He boldly spoke back to the giant. He called out before he knew what was going to happen with faith and trust in His God!!!

David was bold!!

Let's put on Our Armor that the Lord has given us and stand Spiritually and physically against any giant Satan sends our way. Our Lord is well able!!!

We give God the glory! The battle is the Lord's! When the giant sticks it's head up and runs its mouth, cut it off with the Word of God.

STAND BOLDLY like DAVID!!!

EIGHTY-THREE

Psalms 150:2-6

Praise Him for His powerful acts;
Praise Him for His abundant greatness.

Praise Him with trumpet blast;
Praise Him with harp and lyre.

Praise Him with tambourine and dance;
Praise Him with flute and strings.

Praise Him with resounding cymbals;
Praise Him with clashing cymbals.

Let everything that breathes praise the Lord.

Hallelujah!!
In Jesus name Amen

Praise is action!!
Now let's see action!!!

Sadness flees!!
Try it!!

GOD WANTS YOU TO GET YOUR PRAISE ON!!
If EVERYONE did this all day long, oh what a
day for our LORD! He is so worthy!!

EIGHTY-FOUR

Matthew 6: 31-34

Therefore do not worry, 'What shall we eat?' or 'What shall we drink?' or 'What shall we wear?' For after all these things the Gentiles seek. For your heavenly Father knows that you need all these things.
But seek first the kingdom of God and His righteousness, and all these things shall be added to you.
Therefore do not worry about tomorrow, for tomorrow will worry about its own things. Sufficient for the day is its own trouble.

In Jesus name Amen

This is a hard one! I always think to myself: "if God is telling me something, it's for my own good!" (This does take time to learn.) Satan will keep attacking in this area to keep us falling short! WORRY CAUSES SICKNESS!

I've made the decision that I WILL TRUST MY LORD!!!

How many times does Jesus say, "DO NOT?" I know my Lord is true to HIS WORDS, and it is settled!! When a chance comes to worry, I open my lifeline book (MY BIBLE) and I stir myself up!! Stay stirred up. God's words will get you through any situation. DO NOT WORRY. When we get to this point, we can laugh in Satan's face. And another chain that had us in bondage is broken!! Always find a Christian who will agree with the Word of God with you. Seek God first then all things are added to you. If you are seeking God's Kingdom, it's a done deal!

ALL THINGS ARE ADDED TO YOU!!! DON'T WORRY ABOUT TODAY OR TOMORROW!

Bye-bye Satan, you liar! Satan makes you feel, if you don't worry, you don't care!! Oh, what a lie.

When we believe God, we don't worry.

EIGHTY-FIVE

Romans 8:31

What shall we then say to these things? If God be for us, who can be against us?

In Jesus name Amen

What situation are you in? What are you saying to it? Yes, talking to your problem and telling it what to do. What shall we say to these ugly things?

I say: "Satan, I tell you to SHUT UP and HEAR the WORDS MY LORD gave me!! I don't speak my words; I speak the Lord's words! If God is for me, who can be against me???"

Born-again, I am God's! God is for me 100%!!! I take a stand! Who do you think you are, Satan?!

Let's stop playing church and take a strong spiritual stand and be who God says we are!!! God calls you His ambassador; a person who acts as a representative or promoter of a specified activity.

Know who you are and know how much power you have because God has given you the Holy Spirit. No more being bullied by Satan, we know

who you are, and we know you lose in the
end!!!

EIGHTY-SIX

Isaiah 14:16

Those who see you will stare at you. They will ponder you, saying, "Is this the man who made the earth tremble, who shook kingdoms?"

In Jesus name Amen

When we see Satan, we will say: "this is who made me fear, this is who made me doubt, this is who made me sick?" We need to see Satan the way God sees him.

Let's look spiritually at ourselves like God sees us!! The HOLY SPIRIT lives in us, WE ARE THE ONES WHO ARE POWERFUL!!!

We let Satan bully us. Let's stand on God's Word and resist him and he will flee from us!!!

EIGHTY-SEVEN

Psalms 145:1-2

I will extol thee, my God, O King; and I will
bless thy name for ever and ever.
Everyday will I bless thee; and I will praise your
name for ever and ever.

In Jesus name Amen

We are here to please God and worship and
fellowship with him. If men judge the way we
honor our Lord, the way we worship our Lord,
the closeness we have with our Lord, the way
we sing to our Lord, now that is none of our
business! Our business is with the Almighty
God Himself!! Let's honor our King of Kings
today and every day!! Jump out of the box of
tradition and worship your very own way. You
are free to dance, sing, praise, and clap. He is
worthy of ALL our praises!!!

Praise is a powerful weapon. In the Old
Testament, they sent in a praise team before
the fighting began. Start your day with strong
praise and knock Satan back off you for a
while. When you feel the attack again, start
your praise again. While Satan is fighting you
during the day, you sing your day away!! Who
has won? You!!!

EIGHTY-EIGHT

2 Timothy 1:6-7

For this reason I remind you to stir up the gift of God, which is in you through the laying on of my hands.
For God hath not given us the spirit of fear; but of POWER, and of LOVE, and of a sound mind.

In Jesus name Amen

You have been given a gift from God. Step out and listen to the Holy Spirit. Be bold with your gift and always be in love. Always remember God has given you a spirit of POWER and of LOVE. Don't let the spirit of fear stop the gift inside you. (The spirit of fear has not been given to you by God.)

My experience is to keep your mind and eyes on God and fight off the idea of what man will think of you, step out. It's not easy but you must not let Satan stop you in your gifts.

The power is all God's, not any of ours.

ALL GLORY BELONGS TO GOD!!!

EIGHTY-NINE

1 Peter 2:24

Who his own self bare our sins in his own body on the tree, that we, being dead to sins, should live unto righteousness: by whose stripes ye were healed.

In Jesus name Amen

I stood on this verse every day before any illness hit me. When the doctor told me he saw something in my pancreas, I went straight to God and fell on my knees and God spoke to me, He told me to tell no one, that I had no room for any doubt but to stand on this verse and thank Him every day that I AM HEALED!! That's just what I did. Soon the doctor called me and told me to get another MRI. He said that what he saw was bad, it was cancer. This can take a life in months. I went and got another MRI and went back to see my doctor, he was in complete shock to see that the cancer was GONE!!!

It has been 5 years now, as for me I will serve the Lord and I do believe every word my Lord says! I know too much and have seen too much not to believe my Lord!!!

NINETY

John 15:12-15

My command is this: Love each other as I have loved you.
Greater love has no one than this: to lay down one's life for one's friends.
You are my friends if you do what I command. I no longer call you servants because a servant does not know his master's business. You did not choose me, but I chose you and appointed you so that you might go and bear fruit – fruit that will last – and so that whatever you ask in my name the Father will give you.

In Jesus name Amen

You are handpicked by God!! You are special and you are loved!! So, with God loving us so much, we are told to love others. Not some, not the ones we like but love ALL. When we really love, we can ask our Father, in Jesus Name and He will give it to us. You must be a son or daughter and know His will so you can ask according to His ways. LOVE is the walk and God honors that.

Remember at times you can love from a distance. God is true to His Word!!!

NINETY-ONE

1 Peter 2:18-19

Servants, be subject to your masters with all respect, not only to the good and gentle but also to the unjust.
For this is a gracious thing, when, mindful of God, one endures sorrows while suffering unjustly.

In Jesus name Amen

I worked in a nursing home in Mt Doria, Florida. My boss of two years decided to retire. This sweet lady honored my wish to have every Sunday off so I could attend church.

A new boss came in and a new assistant. The assistant had no problem letting everyone know that she believed you live the way you want and make yourself happy.

One day my new boss and this assistant called me into the office. The assistant looked at me and said, "it had come to their attention that I had every Sunday off to go to church and that they would not be honoring that arrangement, like the rest of the team, you will be working Sundays." I said to her that the girl who works for me on Sundays really enjoys the extra money. The assistant said: "sorry you have to work Sundays!" I was so MAD!! I looked at my boss and she said, "sorry Penny." I told them I would let them know what I was going to do.

I went straight to God, with tears!! I wanted to quit!! I wanted to go back to work and say, "I quit now" and walk out!! But God gave me this verse. (I really didn't like it at all.) After years of walking with God, I knew I must follow His word and do it His way!! The next day I went to my boss and asked her for a meeting. I told her I did go to God, and I was to honor her. I even gave her the verse. Much to my surprise she started crying and came over to hug me. She told me that she was so sorry, but the assistant would not let it go and pushed that meeting on her. I did decide to stay and in me doing so, more than forty people who lived in that nursing home accepted Jesus Christ. People who were 80 and 90 years of age. God had a plan!!!

I asked God to forgive me because I really wanted to walk away and feed my flesh. God's way is ALWAYS the best! Humble, meek, submissive.

Satan tried to get me out of there, but Satan can't come against the Word of God and win!!

God's way is PERFECT!! Praise God!!!!

NINETY-TWO

Mark 7:9

And He said unto them, full well ye reject the commandment of God, that ye may keep your own tradition.

In Jesus name Amen

Tradition: passing on customs or beliefs from generation to generation.

You have no idea why you do them. Where is God in church tradition? God has been taken out of some churches and man has placed his own rules and regulations.

Let them come as they are and let Jesus change them. We are to love them and tell them about the good news!!!

When I was little, I went to a church that was full of man's tradition. We had a group of five kids that loved God and were hungry for more. Yes, they came without shoes, and they lived in the country. On rainy days they would have mud on their feet. As I sat smiling, I was so glad to see them because they were my friends. I heard whispers that were not kind. I saw adults shaking their heads at the children.

Where was the love to help wash their feet? (This would have been a suitable time to share a story of Jesus washing feet.) Where was the love to hug these kids and love on them? I was only a kid myself and felt something not right inside this house of God. The tradition to wear certain clothes, a tradition that you had to look a certain way. I think God smiled more on those kids for coming with love in their hearts for Him!

Tradition saves no one!!! Invite all people to come to His house and no matter how they look or smell, we should love them. Those kids felt the judgment and fell away from God.

Let's do things God's way, not man's way. Let's honor our Lord with love!

NINETY-THREE

Psalms 46:10

Be still and know that I am God: I will be
exalted among the heathen, I will be exalted in
the earth.

In Jesus name Amen

Today, really BE STILL. Doing nothing, saying
nothing, and seeing nothing. Just you and God.
He is wanting to talk to you today and every
day. We make time for everything and for other
people, let's make time for our KING.

Oh, how He loves you!!!

NINETY-FOUR

Jeremiah 1:5

Before I formed thee in the belly I knew thee; and before thou camest forth out of the womb I sanctified thee, and I ordained thee a prophet unto the nations.

In Jesus name Amen

Like I said yesterday, I have always felt God and loved Him since I was a child. As I grew into a teen and then an adult, I only wanted God when I needed Him. I was a taker and gave Him nothing back. As a small child, my grandma played a big part in teaching me who God was. (Thank you, God, for giving us Praying Grandma's!!) When I sat with grandma, on one of her weaker days, I could tell she was slowly leaving me. Grandma was hugging me and crying. I asked her, "why are you crying? It's ok, Heaven will be awesome!" She said, "I'm not crying because I am going home, I'm crying because I don't know who is going to carry on God's work in our family when I die." I told her, "Me either grandma." About two weeks later, my sweet grandma passed away. I went into her room and grabbed her big white Bible and sat in the middle of her bed, crying so hard. I heard a voice and stopped crying to hear that voice again. I knew it was God! I listened and heard God say, "remember that question your grandma asked you?" I answered, "yes!" God said, "it is you, Penny!" I jumped up, slammed that Bible back on the shelf and yelled to God, "NO, IT IS NOT ME!!" I ran from God, but because of God's love and mercy here I am serving the Lord with all my heart!

Thank you, Father, for following me and even carrying me. It is an honor to serve the LORD! God gave me His Son. Why did I run and hide from someone who loves me so much? Why did I run to the world that cares nothing for me? Is God speaking to you? I say: YES, HE IS!!

NINETY-FIVE

Hebrews 11:1

Now faith is the substance of things hoped for, the evidence of things not seen.

In Jesus name Amen

In my testimonies, I always protect the person's name. But I have decided not to in this testimony. I am going to start with the end of the story.

My earthly father was born again before he passed. He was so loved by all his children, and we still honor him today!! He was loving and so caring. My father would feel honored that I spoke about him to help others. He would be proud of that.

Now for the rest of my testimony:

My father drank a lot. My father liked to party and was violent when he drank. As a child I knew God, I could feel His presence and as a child, I was hungry for more of God. When I found this verse, I stood on this verse - faith in my God and hope I had for my father to change his heart. I once told someone that I prayed for my daddy every day, and that God was going to help my dad. My hope in this was so strong! That person told me, "You can stop praying for him because there is NO HOPE for him." I would not waver, I always said my prayer every night and then in my thirties, six months before he passed, my daddy gave his heart to God and was born-again!

My dad stopped drinking! My dad stopped his partying! My dad's heart was changed! My dad was so sweet, kind and loving!

Oh, that person saw the change in my dad and said, "I guess there is always hope for people."

Never give up hope for people. Far and near, always pray for them. Don't ever give up your hope and your faith in God!! Life and death are in the words you use. Speak life into someone and pray always!!

You cannot change someone, but with God nothing is impossible.

See you soon Daddy!!

NINETY-SIX

Matthew 22:36-39

Master, which is the great commandment in the law?
Jesus said unto him, "Thou shalt love the Lord thy God with all thy heart, and with all thy soul, and with all thy mind."
"This is the first and great commandment."
"And the second is like unto it, Thou shalt love thy neighbor as thyself."

In Jesus name Amen

My heart desires to live the way God has set before me, not my own ways, but His. As I have grown, I have learned that when I do things God's way, my life does turn out better! Now all of this did not happen at once. It is a journey and small steps at a time. This is a journey to please God. It's not trying to get Him to love me more. God already sent His Son to die for me while I was still a sinner. That's a true love that goes so deep.

I really had a hard time praying for this one person, and God says to love them. Really!! But the answer is yes!!

In my prayer, I would say to God "please bless _____ because YOU want me to pray for her." Every night that's how I ended my prayer. This went on for about a year. Then one day I closed my eyes and said, "Lord I pray that you bless _____ because I really want you to bless her." I didn't even know when my heart changed for her, but it did. As my eyes were closed, I saw God and from His heart to my heart were the whitest of lights that I had ever seen. It was so warm, and I could feel this strong LOVE go into my heart. As I retell this story, I can feel it all over again. Then God spoke, "Penny, now you understand my unconditional LOVE! Always love everyone with this love you feel right now!" Of course, I could do nothing but cry. I did not have a social life with her. I didn't have to spend time with her. I only had to LOVE her God's way.

I look at people differently now. No matter who they are, God did send His son to die for them. God did change a stone heart to a caring and loving heart. Walk God's way! He will help you change; you don't change yourself.

I lift my God up always. I will dance before Him! I will shout before Him! I will cry before Him! I know what He has done for me!!! My expression is for my LORD and only for my LORD. It is from the deepest part of my heart!!

NINETY-SEVEN

Philippians 4:19-20

But my God shall supply all your need according to his riches in glory by Jesus Christ. Now unto God and our Father by glory for ever and ever.

In Jesus name Amen

I will share my experiences and I am here to say OUR GOD is FAITHFUL to HIS WORD!!

I was in a situation that I was responsible for putting myself in. Knowing the Lord and not really living for Him completely. I was a lukewarm Christian. I would party and drink hard on Friday and Saturday nights then off to church on Sunday. I was lukewarm for the Lord by my own choice. Not knowing what I was going to do, I did know to run to the Lord, and I said this verse over and over out loud with tears, to the Lord. It really was hard for me to believe and have faith in His Word. My Lord had love and compassion for me. I needed a place to move to. I did let people know that I was moving and that I had nothing to put into the apartment I had just rented.

Some people called and told me to stop by and pick up this and that. So, the person who drove the truck rental decided to map out where people lived and a way we went. After all the stops we ended our trip at the apartment I rented. We unloaded the truck. I sat in the corner crying! Really crying!! My Lord was faithful!! As I looked around, all my rooms were full of anything that a kitchen, bedroom, bathroom, living room, and dining room needed. It all was like new and looked like I picked it all out myself!!

GOD just supplied ALL MY NEEDS!! KEEP YOUR FAITH IN GOD! HE IS FAITHFUL! No longer am I a lukewarm Christian, I am hot for the LORD!!!

NINETY-EIGHT

Romans 12:17-20

Recompense to no man evil for evil. Provide things honest in the sight of all men.
If it be possible, as much as lieth in you, live peaceably with all men.
Dearly beloved, avenge not yourselves, but rather give place unto wrath: for it is written, vengeance is mine; I will repay, saith the Lord.
Therefore is thine enemy hunger, feed him; if he thirst, give him drink: for in so doing thou shalt heap coals of fire on his head.

In Jesus name Amen

We may not understand these words, but His words are for us, not against us. This is why we walk by faith not by sight or emotions. Let's do as Our Father tells us! We don't need to hang with people when they are so mean to us but live in peace.

I have given water to someone who has cussed me out. I have taken food to their door because I heard they were sick and needed food. My flesh was screaming at me, don't give her anything!! As I stood at her door and knocked, I wanted to run!! She opened the door and took the food. She asked me why I was being nice to her. I wanted to say I really don't want to be, but when I opened my mouth the words "God loves you and cares for you" came out. "God told me to give to you when I see a need with you." She started crying and soon she was going to church, and another soul was saved from hell.

God does know better than we do. Trust Him and stay in peace and God will change things and turn things around. It may not be overnight, but IT WILL HAPPEN.

Why did I follow God's Word instead of my feelings? His way is only the best for me, no matter how hard it is to obey His Words. This lady has passed, but now when I think of her, I smile! I thank God for helping me step by step with doing things His Way!!!

NINETY-NINE

Romans 5:8

But God shows his love for us in that while we were still sinners, Christ died for us.

In Jesus name Amen

You don't have to clean yourself up to go before God. Come just as you are. While you were still a sinner, Jesus died for you.

That's LOVE!!

Renew YOUR LOVE for Jesus. Tell him every chance you get today how much you love Him. We can never tell Him enough how much we love Him!!

ONE HUNDRED

Psalms 147:3

He heals the brokenhearted and binds up their wounds.

In Jesus name Amen

God sees all and He is taking care of our broken hearts and our wounds. God is quick to come to the aid of all those whose hearts are broken and wounded for He is the God of all comfort.

ONE HUNDRED ONE

James 1:12

Blessed is the man who remains steadfast under trial, for when he has stood the test he will receive the crown of life, which God has promised to those who love him.

In Jesus name Amen

Endure: Suffer (something painful or difficult) patiently.

Yes, at times it is hard, we can Endure!!! Keep your eyes on Jesus. Look for that verse that talks about your situation. God has given a way for us to endure, and it's not the world's way to endure.

YES, you can endure, JESUS IS WITH YOU ALWAYS!!

ONE HUNDRED TWO

Isaiah 40:29-31

He gives power to the faint, and to him who has no might he increases strength.
Even youths shall faint and be weary, and young men shall fall exhausted;
but they who wait for the Lord shall renew their strength; they shall mount up with wings like eagles; they shall run and not be weary; they shall walk and not faint.

In Jesus name Amen

God gives power and strength. He renews. What do you need this day? Have a seat with God and receive what He has already given. He gave Jesus and Jesus gave it ALL to you!!! Build yourself up with the Word of God and KNOW that HE HAS ALREADY GIVEN YOU everything!!!

Now speak it over yourself!! The truth!!

Speak what God speaks over you!

God does not lie!! There is life and death in our very own words!!!

ONE HUNDRED THREE

Proverbs 18:10

The name of the LORD is a strong tower; the righteous run to it and are safe.

In Jesus name Amen

No matter what situation you are in, when you STOP and TURN and RUN to the LORD, you are SAFE. If your problem seems to be over your head, THE LORD IS TALLER!!!

ONE HUNDRED FOUR

John 8:36

So if the Son sets you free, you will be free indeed.

In Jesus name Amen

Jesus has set us free from so many different things. Jesus died, took our sin, our weakness, and our sicknesses. It's hard for us to understand how much He took on Himself so that you would not keep holding on to stuff that makes your heart heavy. As you grow in the Lord and read His word, you will see and know that Jesus did so much when He died. When we die, we die and if we are born-again, we go to Heaven. Jesus spiritually TOOK so much on Himself to GIVE you freedom from ALL things.

If you are feeling guilty about something, go to Jesus and confess it and ask forgiveness. You don't beg God to forgive you!! Just ask and turn away from it.

YOU ARE SO FREE. Any guilt is from Satan. That's that heavy feeling you feel. God will gently touch you and let you know you don't have to carry this anymore.

Today, let's realize how much He has set us free from. You're not a prisoner any longer to sin, sickness, or any guilt. You are free indeed.

Walk strong and walk with a smile!!!

Jesus has given you a white gown to wear now and forever. Don't keep the old rags on!! You are new in Jesus, and it fits us all!!!

ONE HUNDRED FIVE

Hebrews 10:23

Let us hold fast the confession of our hope without wavering, for He who promised is faithful.

In Jesus name Amen

Hold on dearly to God's Word! He is a true and living God. When things happen, don't think differently of your God. Yes! He is faithful to ALL His promises.

Don't waver...being undecided about the world's way or God's way. God says hold fast to THE CONFESSION OF OUR HOPE. Your faith is the substances HOPED for, the evidence of things not seen. Again, God is faithful to carry out ALL His promises.

You don't have to understand everything with God, just believe, trust and have faith in His word. If you find yourself wavering, stop and put your eyes on Jesus. You know in your heart that He is faithful. Read His wonderful words when you feel down, and they will lift you up while you're waiting. Keep saying out loud His Word until your whole atmosphere is full and your joy is back!!

ONE HUNDRED SIX

1 Corinthians 10:10

And do not grumble, (complain) as some of them did - and were killed by the destroyer.

In Jesus name Amen

Yes, our Lord has Mercy and Love!!

If we are going to talk about the Word of God, we will take it all and not just some of the Word. We need to have all the pieces of God's Word like a puzzle. We can't throw out the pieces we don't like because to see His plan we need all the pieces. Complaining is not of God. The old testimony is our example of the whole puzzle. They complained, they lusted after evil things (not always sex), and they worshipped other things than God. They partied and partied and said there is no God and picked what and how they would live. Boy did they get their reward! In one day 23,000 fell!! Some died by serpents.

Our God loves us and tells us and shows us how to walk after Him. Let's stop doing what most of us do, complaining. That could very well stop our blessing. Replace the complaining with FAITH. Really, if we trust God, what do we have to complain about? Those who stand and trust will have a great reward from God!!

Venting to a friend is not a form of complaining. We need each other to help us along the way. But stop there and take Godly wisdom. Then trust in your Father!!

ONE HUNDRED SEVEN

1 Corinthians 10:13

No temptation has overtaken you that is not common to man. God is faithful, and he will not let you be tempted beyond your ability, but with the temptation, he will also provide the way of escape, that you may be able to endure it.

In Jesus name Amen

Be ENCOURAGED today that God knows and sees what you are going through. Know in your heart you can trust your LORD!! With God, He makes a way for you to escape it and endure it. Will you be tempted? YES! Satan will always find a situation to put into your path that will tempt you not to trust God. God is there with you, and He is the one that will give you the ability to get through it and endure it!! The Holy Spirit is your helper! Hey, you will get through it! You will become stronger, and you will grow with God. The Lord never said it will only take a day, a week or any time limit, just close your eyes take a deep breath, and THANK GOD that HE HAS MADE A WAY FOR YOU. Picture yourself holding His hand. Now WALK IT OUT. Oh, what a testimony you will have to help others!!

ONE HUNDRED EIGHT

Matthew 9:13

But go and learn what this means: "I desire mercy, not sacrifice. For I have not come to call the righteous, but sinners."

In Jesus name Amen

As we walk into our church on Sunday, we always try to do as Jesus did. Let's not forget the one main thing with God, that he sent His SON to save a sinner. So, as we walk into work or school and see the world act ugly with their ways, their actions, their attitudes, remember Jesus came and gave His life for them!! He did for me also. How about you?

Let's win the sinner over to God and let God clean them up. Don't get mad at them, they haven't met Jesus yet. That's why you are where you are. Let the light shine from you and they will come to you when they have trouble or when they need prayer. Be ready with open arms like Jesus is.

THAT'S WHY HE CAME!!!

ONE HUNDRED NINE

2 Corinthians 4:8-9

We are hard-pressed on every side, yet not crushed; we are perplexed, but not in despair; perplexed, but not forsaken; struck down, but not destroyed.

In Jesus name Amen

Yes, we will walk through the valley!
We walk through all things with the Lord beside us, in us, and guiding us!

We are not CRUSHED,

We are not IN DESPAIR,

We are not FORSAKEN,

We are not DESTROYED.

Yes, things get tough, but we have good news in the Word of God.
Quitting is not an option!
God has you in His hands. You will get through it!!
Believe and keep walking in Faith!

ONE HUNDRED TEN

Psalms 37:17

For the arms of the wicked shall be broken: but the Lord upholdeth the righteous.

In Jesus name Amen

Jesus made us RIGHTEOUS, RIGHT STANDING. So, take your true position when you stand in front of your God. There is nothing you can do in your own ability to be righteous. Jesus took the nails and shed His blood to make sure we can stand in front of God in a white gown. What a great gift!!

THIS IS ME AND YES, THAT'S YOU ALSO!!! HE LOVES YOU BEYOND ANYTHING YOU CAN MEASURE!!

ONE HUNDRED ELEVEN

Ephesians 6:14-17

Stand firm then, with the belt of truth buckled
around your waist, with the breastplate of
righteousness in place,
and with your feet fitted with the readiness that
comes from the gospel of peace.
In addition to all this, take of the shield of
faith, with which you can extinguish all the
flaming arrows of the evil one.
Take the helmet of salvation and the sword of
the Spirit, which is the word of God.

In Jesus name Amen

How do you stand against Satan? With
everything he is not!! He does not understand
the things of God.

TRUTH

RIGHTEOUSNESS

PEACE

FAITH

SALVATION

WORD OF GOD

God has given you the perfect outfit to wear!! Don't go naked. Spiritually He has equipped you, it's up to you to put this on, and when you do, it will do what the Lord says it will do!! You are exposed to the schemes of Satan if you choose to walk without your spiritual clothes.

God is a gentleman; He will not force you to use wisdom. It's important to wear your clothes every day, all day, not just when you want to wear them. DO NOT EXPOSE YOURSELF TO SATAN. Even in the desert, Jesus showed us how this works. He is our example.

ONE HUNDRED TWELVE

1 Corinthians 13: 4-8

Love is patient, love is kind. It does not envy, it does not boast, it is not proud. It does not dishonor others, it is not self-seeking, it is not easily angered, it keeps no record of wrongs. Love does not delight in evil but rejoices with the truth. It always protects, always trusts, always hopes, always perseveres. Love never fails. But where there are prophecies, they will cease; where there are tongues, they will be stilled; where there is knowledge, it will pass away.

In Jesus name Amen

Our Lord does not want us to pick and choose how to LOVE each other. Here is our list. Maybe today we should work on our love walk toward each other. Not for some people you know but for all people.

ONE HUNDRED THIRTEEN

Isaiah 53:5

But he was wounded for our transgressions, he was bruised for our iniquities: the chastisement of our peace was upon him; and with his stripes we are healed.

In Jesus name Amen

It was planned!

It was written!

It was carried out!

Don't fight to get your healing!

Fight to keep it!

Satan came to steal, kill, and destroy.

Satan comes to steal your healing.

If he STEALS your healing, he can kill you!

He can destroy you!

With the Grace of God and our Faith, my words are yes, I am healed, and I am keeping my healing!! Why? Because God is the one who said, "I am healed before I was born."

ONE HUNDRED FOURTEEN

Psalms 18:2

The Lord is my rock, and my fortress, and my deliverer; my God, my strength, in whom I will trust; my buckler, and the horn of my salvation, and my high tower.

In Jesus name Amen

Are you going through stuff? You're tired of it! Guess what? Believe it or not, you are so blessed. Sometimes we look through the wrong eyes, human eyes. But really, sometimes you must stop and look through your spiritual eyes. This is where the truth really is.

You must be on the right track with God because Satan is always knocking you down, but you keep getting back up!! You GO! You are the one who is making a difference in this life for Jesus!!! God is your deliverer!!

Satan is more afraid of you when you work unto the Lord. Satan sees what you are doing for God and wants you to stop.
Read and reread this verse. God has already planned your delivery from what is going on with you. Go ahead and praise Him, laugh out loud with tears!! You are not alone, my friend!

ONE HUNDRED FIFTEEN

Psalms 15:1-5

Lord, who may dwell in your sacred tent?

Who may live on your holy mountain?

The one whose walk is blameless,

Who does what is righteous,

Who speaks the truth from their heart:

whose tongue utters no slander,

Who does no wrong to a neighbor,

And casts no slur on others:

who despises a vile person

But honors those who fear the Lord;

Who keeps an oath even when it hurts,

And does not change their mind;

who lends money to the poor without interest;

Who does not accept a bribe against the innocent.

In Jesus name Amen

ONE HUNDRED SIXTEEN

Romans 8:37

Yet in all these things we are more than a conqueror through Him who loves us.

In Jesus name Amen

No matter what you are going through you are told by God who you are and what you can do through Christ. If you are walking by faith, if you draw near to God each day, if you have a relationship with Him, then you are MORE THAN A CONQUEROR who will successfully overcome (a problem or weakness). Do you believe the word of God? NOW ACT LIKE IT!!

You can overcome anything; you and the Lord make an amazing team! Keep His word in your heart, about yourself. The Lord sees who you really are. Now it's time that you see who you really are!!

NOT LESS, NOT SOMEWHAT, but MORE than a CONQUEROR!

ONE HUNDRED SEVENTEEN

Hebrews 3:14-15

For we have become partakers of Christ if we
hold the beginning of our confidences
steadfastly to the end.
While it is said: "Today if you hear His voice, do
not harden your hearts as in rebellion."

In Jesus name Amen

Today when you stand for God, make sure you
really are standing for Him and not against
Him. The world has one way and God has His
way. Which way do you really choose? Just
because you may not understand God's way
does not mean it's of the devil. Don't mix
education with the Spirit world. God will guide
you when your mind can not understand. This
is called FAITH and TRUST. Use the Word of
God to show you what is of Him and what is of
the world.

Walk with wisdom from God!

ONE HUNDRED EIGHTEEN

Mark 9:1

And He said to them, Assuredly, I say to you that there are some standing here who will not taste death till they see the kingdom of God present with power.

In Jesus name Amen

Jesus is coming, but will it be in this generation? No one knows!! Jesus tells us to be ready!! Choose this day to turn to Jesus. Do you have time tomorrow to come to Jesus? Tomorrow is not promised! One step away from God is two steps too many and puts you in the middle of hell forever. Be the one who asks God into your heart today and ask for forgiveness. So easy but yet SO powerful! Yes, life is in the power of YOUR tongue.

ONE HUNDRED NINETEEN

Isaiah 28:23

Give ear and hear my voice.

Listen and hear my voice.

In Jesus name Amen

Does God speak to you?

Yes, but first we need to do something.

That is GIVE our ear. Know that He does speak to you in many ways.

Listen, stop talking, and now listen for His voice. Have time in this crazy world and give an ear and listen to what He is telling you. He is telling you this very day because He is speaking to you!

ONE HUNDRED TWENTY

Isaiah 5:20

Woe to those who call evil good and good evil, who put darkness for light and light for darkness, who put bitter for sweet and sweet for bitter.

In Jesus name Amen
When Jesus came on the scene, people had to shift to a new way of learning and teaching His Word. His Word is still the same, but He gives people new ideas to help let go of things that enslave us. Know that God will show us a way that is passed our understanding. Listen and hear what the Holy Spirit is saying. The main thing is people are drawn to God in Jesus name. People will be changed for the good to give Glory to God. Don't be a hard-hearted Christian and stand in the way of our God. Don't call a new thing evil that God is using to free people.

God says woe to you. God always gives a warning. Check your heart. Check that you are in line with God's moving Spirit. Something new is not always evil. Jesus was not evil! Jesus is the best thing that ever happened to and for us! Don't judge! No matter if it's singing in a new way, dancing unto the Lord or renewing your relationship with the

Lord on a deeper level. Let's move forward with
OUR LORD!!

ONE HUNDRED TWENTY-ONE

Psalms 29:11

The Lord will give strength to His people; The Lord will bless His people with peace.

In Jesus name Amen

Ok, how do you stop WORRY and get this PEACE from God? Feed your FAITH with what God says. We all know what worry is! Stop right then and say: "I trust you Father, here is why my flesh wants to WORRY: _____. I will say out loud for my ears to hear what you have just told me in Your Word, YOU WILL bless your people with peace." When I hand them over first, then by faith I will walk away with peace. Each worry thought in my mind is a sign for me to stop and tell God about it.

God is your everything, don't walk around in torment when He has given you the way out. You must make this choice and when you do, you will live by it. Will you allow yourself to be chained or allow yourself to be free from worry? You must go to the Lord! Faith stops Satan and moves the hand of God. Worry gives Satan power because there is no faith. Believe OUR GOD! Strength and peace, He gives to you!

ONE HUNDRED TWENTY-TWO

Matthew 6:27

Can any one of you by worrying add a single hour to your life?

In Jesus name Amen

A great question!

God has nothing to do with worry. When you start to worry, God says NO!! If our Lord tells us that worry is not good, we should run the other way. If it is not from God, then it's from Satan. Satan makes us believe that if we don't worry, we don't care! God says also give Him all our cares. We are to stand with a confident smile, knowing God is taking care of all our concerns. We must hand them over to Him and ask Him and then not wait to see the answer but act by faith that He has already done it for us.

Today is a new day! A new way to do things! If worry comes, thank God for taking it and shake Satan off!! Worry is not for God's Christians. Worry is an empty shell and there you stand with it and Satan is laughing. Replace the worry with a verse from God. His Words always work!!!

ONE HUNDRED TWENTY-THREE

Psalms 27:13

I believe that I shall look upon the goodness of the Lord in the land of the living!

In Jesus name Amen

When things get us down, let's look all around and see the goodness that the Lord has given to us, right here where we are. Today only pick the good stuff that is all around you. Start with the little things that sometimes we overlook. All good things are from God.

Be happy and enjoy this day!!

ONE HUNDRED TWENTY-FOUR

Revelation 22:20

He (Jesus) who testifies to these things says, "SURELY I AM COMING QUICKLY."

Amen, Even so, come Lord Jesus!

In Jesus name Amen

We do not know when or the time of Jesus' return. We do not know if one will live or be with the Lord today or tomorrow. When He comes, it will be quickly.

Today is the day to clean your heart and read His word. Really get to know your God NOW! Pattycake days are over! Attention every born-again Christian: don't be lukewarm with your God. We have Grace and Mercy NOW. If you know people who are not born-again, remember where they will be if the Lord comes today. Give mercy to those who do not deserve it and be so sweet and kind and win them over to the Lord. Start today and work on that one person that gets on your nerves the most. Hell is real and you must care if they will burn there forever!! Can you look into their eyes as they burn and say that you do not care? No, you cannot!! Hell is more real than your home or your job. He comes quickly!!! God has you where you are because He is trusting you with the people that come into your life on this day. God's Words are here to guide us, to show love, to show mercy, to love on us, to correct us, and to keep us real with the life to come. Today, hear what the Spirit is saying. No rolling of the eyes to people, that will not win them to the Lord. Time is near and we should be about our Father's business.

ONE HUNDRED TWENTY-FIVE

Luke 23:36

Watch ye therefore, and pray always, that ye may be accounted worthy to escape all these things that shall come to pass, and to stand before the Son of man.

In Jesus name Amen

Always...without fail, consistently, unfailingly.

We need to pray in truth and honesty to our Lord. There is wisdom in this verse. Things are coming that we know not, but our God knows it and is giving us wisdom. Start today in a prayer that is faithful. Stay in God's Word and stay strong! Things are coming! Watch and pray that you may be counted worthy to escape these things.

Be happy, share His word and be ready to stand on His word without the Bible in your hands. Have His powerful words in your heart. What you have in your heart will come out of your mouth. Walk in faith and always believe the words of God that you say! Born-again Christians let's be ready for all things.

ONE HUNDRED TWENTY-SIX

2 Timothy 1:9

He has saved us and called us to a holy life –
not because of anything we have done but
because of his own purpose and grace. This
grace was given to us in Christ Jesus before the
beginning of time.

In Jesus name Amen

You are loved by the greatest! He called you to
Him! He knew all about you before the
beginning of time began! You are someone
special to the Lord! He chooses you to do His
work! He gave you grace! He has equipped you
with everything you need: The Holy Spirit! YOU
ARE the one for the job. He gave you a book to
follow to make sure you do the job His way and
in His purpose. While you are in the world at
that job, there is an inside job that only you can
do. You have been called. The Lord will guide
you on this mission.

Born again children, get your armor on and
move forward!!

ONE HUNDRED TWENTY-SEVEN

Psalms 8:4-6

What is mankind that you are mindful of them,
human beings that you care for them?
You have made them a little lower than the
angels and crowned them with glory and
honor.
You made them rulers over the works of your
hands; you put everything under their feet.

In Jesus name Amen

You are so loved by GOD! God has crowned you
and He honors you. Born-again Christian, I'm
talking to you! Don't think lower of yourself.
You are someone! Yes, you are important! God
calls you His own and makes you a ruler over
His works. Take your position!! The King of all
has made you and called you to do His work!!
He is trusting you today. With honor and a
crown of glory, now THAT IS LOVE. Just sit and
think about this today. The King of Kings, The
Lord above all sees YOU for who you really are!

Wake up each morning knowing who you really
are. You are loved, truly loved by the perfect
one. Walk by God's standard, not yours and not
the worlds. You are the new and born again
best of you!!

ONE HUNDRED TWENTY-EIGHT

Matthew 4:10

Then saith Jesus unto him, Get thee hence, Satan: for it is written, Thou shalt worship the Lord thy God, and him only shalt thou serve.

In Jesus name Amen

Jesus was here to teach us and show us the way. Don't find it strange that Satan attacks you, he also attacked Jesus, but we don't just stand by and let Satan have his way with us. You take the authority to speak and tell him to leave. You do it in Jesus name. The GREATER one lives in you. Step forward and speak and remove Satan from your situation. Know who lives in you, The Holy Spirit!! There is a war against good and evil. Take the authority that has been given to you and win your battle.

YOU SPEAK in the name of your King, who is with you every moment of every day!!!

ONE HUNDRED TWENTY-NINE

Psalms 118:24

This is the day the Lord has made; we will rejoice and be glad in it.

In Jesus name Amen

REJOICE...show great joy or delights.

GLAD...pleased.

Have joy and great pleasure today!

This day was made for YOU from God!

Remember not just to have great joy and pleasure but show it!!!

ONE HUNDRED THIRTY

James 2:17

In the same way, faith by itself, if it is not accompanied by action, is dead.

In Jesus name Amen

When you have faith in God, there is always action that comes after your faith. When you walk by faith you are moving forward. That is your action. When you have faith and hear His voice you DO what He tells you. Doing is the action.

What is faith without your action? It is dead! Faith does not stand by itself, and neither should you. You should not just read your Bible and keep what you learn to yourself. By your faith, you open your mouth and share the Word of God with others. It is not just you or about you anymore.

Look at my works and I will show you my faith. Because of my faith, I have stepped out and acted on God's word. You will see great faith when you see people's works. You are not saved by your works alone. You have pleased your Lord, your God! You have let your light shine to others because of your faith and works. You see someone in need of something, but you ignore it, faith without works is dead. Your faith makes you step out. You see someone in need and ask if you can help or jump in and help. That's faith and works! Faith that God has led you to that person for a reason. Your works is showing you trust God and you help without any payback.

ONE HUNDRED THIRTY-ONE

Acts 7:59-60

And they stoned Stephen, (Stephen walked with Jesus) calling upon God, and saying, Lord Jesus, receive my spirit.
Then he fell on his knees and cried out, "Lord do not hold this sin against them." When he had said this, he fell asleep.

In Jesus name Amen

Has someone hurt you or someone you love? Look what Saul did, he killed people just for following Jesus and being a Christian. God turned this hard-hearted man (Saul, now known as Paul, who writes most of the New Testament), into one He could use for His Kingdom. God says pray for our enemies.

If God is important to you and you stand for God, then we must pray for our enemies. God can change any of our enemies. Don't let Satan tell you that you have the right to hold anything against people. Do you need to hang out with your enemies? No but you should pray for them! Because you prayed for them and they are changed and now walk on the path to get others saved, this is what it is all about! Didn't Jesus forgive you and now you help others get saved. It's not about you or how they treat you, it's about praying for our enemies and them getting saved; then going out and helping others get saved. It's the domino effect! Let's pray for our enemies because it could change a piece of the world and a lot of souls will go to heaven!! Don't let Satan deceive you into believing you have a right not to forgive. Keeping peace in your heart also keeps the body healthy!

ONE HUNDRED THIRTY-TWO

John 16:33

I have said these things to you, that in me you may have peace. In the world you will have tribulation. But take heart, I have overcome the world.

In Jesus name Amen

Tribulation: Suffering, distress, misery, unhappiness, sadness, heartache.

Jesus has overcome the world!! Jesus tells us to be of good cheer because he also calls us an overcomer! Yes, we will have these things as we follow Jesus, but in a little while it does pass with faith in our Lord. We will overcome it all because with Jesus, we can do all things, ALL things! Do not forget those words: ALL THINGS, THROUGH JESUS CHRIST WHO GIVES US OUR STRENGTH!

Be of good cheer!! Jesus can see what is happening in your life and tells you to be of good cheer. He knows it's all going to work out!! Go ahead and give Him glory now. Take His peace, that is in Jesus, and have confidence as you walk this out!!

ONE HUNDRED THIRTY-THREE

Galatians 6:1-2

Brothers and sisters, if someone is caught in a sin, you who live by the Spirit should restore that person gently. But watch yourselves, or you also may be tempted.
Carry each other's burdens, and in this way you will fulfill the law of Christ.

In Jesus name Amen

Help your brother or sister who has fallen into sin. Listen to the Holy Spirit as He guides you to help get this person back to God. Be gentle because there is temptation all around us and we may fall short of God's Word, and we may need a gentle hand to get us back on track.

ONE HUNDRED THIRTY-FOUR

1 Corinthians 10:13

There hath no temptation taken you but such as is common to man: but God is faithful, who will not suffer you to be tempted above that ye are able; but will with the temptation also make a way to escape, that ye may be able to bare it.

In Jesus name Amen

I WILL BE OKAY!!!

Sing your way through it. Put the praise at the beginning of your morning!!

It will work out better than you could ever think.

God says so!!!!

What else do you need from your Father?!

ONE HUNDRED THIRTY -FIVE

Galatians 5:1

For freedom Christ has set us free; stand firm therefore, and do not submit again to a yoke of slavery.

In Jesus name Amen

Satan will put temptation in front of you and tell you to go ahead and take the temptation. What can it hurt just this once? Then you step back into the situation that God had already taken you out of.

God's Word to you is, do not submit again!!! There is danger!!!

If you give into Satan, you are now back into slavery. Whether it is a big or small thing. You have made the choice. Repent and turn back to God's way and stand firm!! God's Word is wisdom to help you!

ONE HUNDRED THIRTY-SIX

2 Chronicles 20:21

After consulting the people, Jehoshaphat appointed men to sing to the LORD and to praise Him for the splendor of His holiness as they went out at the head of the army, saying; "Give thanks to the LORD, for His love endures forever."

In Jesus name Amen

They won the battle!! Let's do the same in our battles!!

Read this again and again until it really falls into your heart. The Word of the Lord is spiritual. Keep your eyes and ears open and walk in the Lord's word, which is moved by our faith in the spiritual world. The Lord is powerful!!

ONE HUNDRED THIRTY-SEVEN

1 Samuel 2:30

Therefore the LORD, the God of Israel, declares: "I promised that members of your family would minister before me forever." But now the LORD declares, "Far be it from me! Those who honor me I will honor, but those who despise me will be disdained.

In Jesus name Amen

Disdained: considered to be unworthy of one's consideration.

In all your actions, do you honor the Lord? A question to ask yourself NOW, not when you see our Lord. It's all about being real and not just putting on an act for certain people. Do not sugar coat what you do or who you are. Do you honor the Lord in all you do? What do you want from the Lord?

ONE HUNDRED THIRTY-EIGHT

2 Kings 6:1-7

Now the company of prophets said to Elisha,
"As you see, the place where we live under your
charge is too small for us."
"Let us go to the Jordan, and let us collect logs
there, one for each of us to live." He answered,
"Do so."
Then one of them said, "Please come with your
servants." And he answered, "I will."
So he went with them. When they came to the
Jordan, they cut down trees.
But as one was felling a log, his ax head fell into
the water; he cried out, "Alas, master! It was
borrowed."
Then the man of God said, "Where did it fall?"
When he showed him the place, he cut off a
stick, and threw it in there, and made the iron
float.
He said, "Pick it up." So he reached out his hand
and took it.

In Jesus name Amen

Truth...every time I lose something I always say
these verses out loud to God. If He will do it for
them, I know He will do it for me.

God does answer!

Go ahead and walk out in faith with God. Don't doubt. Wait, He will help you every time!

You can take things away from me, but you can't take my experience away that God has given me. I know God answers!!! Who else can do the impossible? No one except our loving Lord!

ONE HUNDRED THIRTY-NINE

2 Timothy 1:13

Hold fast the pattern of sound words which you have heard from me, in faith and love which are in Christ Jesus.

In Jesus name Amen

Recognize that the Word of God is a treasure and a great value. Guard the Word of God. Know that you hold everything you need to live in this world. Do not let the enemy (Satan) tell you it has no power, that the Word of God does not have to be followed. Do not let the enemy tell you that the Word of God is not for today or that you can live however you want. The Word of God is a sound Word and full of joy just for you! If you follow the world, you will soon give up that joy and give your permission to the enemy to make you a slave to this world again. If will always lead you to a false sense of joy.

Hold fast to the truth and the Word of God!! This is the real treasure and the true freedom and the real joy of the Lord. Joy from the Word of God goes into the heart and the joy is not gone just because the situation changes. God's way is the only true way! We are so rich with His Word!

ONE HUNDRED FORTY

Ephesians 5:8-11

For you were once darkness but now you are a
light in the Lord. Walk as children of light.
(For the fruit of the Spirit is in all goodness,
righteousness, and truth)
finding out what is acceptable to the Lord.
and have no fellowship with the unfruitful
works of darkness, but rather expose them.

In Jesus name Amen

Fellowship: To hold something in common.

So, what does light have in common with
darkness? Absolutely NOTHING!!!! Be ready to
be a witness, share God's Word. Don't hang
with darkness or their kind. Do help them with
the Word of God. Bring them to church. Pray for
them. Someone prayed for you when you were
trapped in that darkness. Walk with the light
(Jesus is the light) not darkness (Satan is the
father of darkness). People are blind to the way
of darkness. They need you to show them the
way to the light. Sooner or later that light will
shine so brightly through them because you
took the time for them. You cannot walk in
both the light and the darkness. Which path
will you choose? How will you live? Can the

darkness see that you are different? If not, you don't have anything they need.

Be the someone that is different and live in the open for Jesus no matter who is against the truth! Don't be ashamed to stand on God's Word. You may have to stand against your mom, dad, your kids, your grandkids, husband, wife, or other family or friends. Stand with what the truth is: Jesus!

The sun shines boldly, DO YOU?

ONE HUNDRED FORTY-ONE

Romans 6:6

Knowing this, that our man was crucified with Him. That the body of sin might be done away with, that we should no longer be slave to sin.

In Jesus name Amen

When you were baptized, you were spiritually baptized with Jesus' death. As you go under the water, you are dying to sin! All sin has been washed away. As you come up out of the water you are a new person, you are free from sin! You are now alive to God in Christ Jesus our Lord! Sin has no control over your life any longer! You have chosen to walk with God every day.

Is the opportunity still there to sin? Yes, but Satan has no power over you any longer. Asking God to come into your heart and to be baptized is the road our Lord leads us down. We shout every day that we are no longer a slave to sin!!!

ONE HUNDRED FORTY-TWO

Galatians 6:9

And let us not grow weary while doing good, for in due season we shall reap if we do not lose heart.

In Jesus name Amen

Some days are harder than others. Some days we want to throw in the towel and say forget it!! God knew we would feel like this and to help us, He gave us this word: DO NOT lose heart in doing good.

It's very important for us to stay on track and keep doing good to others because one day we will see the change in people when we do not give up on them. Oh, what a reward that will be. If we don't see it down here, we will see it in Heaven while standing beside our God! Then you will be glad you followed His Word. Do not grow weary while doing good! He sees all that you do for Him and is pleased.

Chin up, eyes on God and do something good today for that person who is not so nice!

ONE HUNDRED FORTY-THREE

Mark 7:9

He (Jesus) said to them (us), "All too well you reject the commandments of God, that you may keep your tradition."

In Jesus name Amen

Tradition: the transmission of customs or beliefs from generation to generation, or the fact of being passed on in this way.

God is not a tradition. You will not find Him in tradition. Follow the Word of God. Man's tradition will carry you far from God. God says sing and shout unto Him, but tradition has taught you to be silent in church. There are a lot of traditions that you need to change for God, which is something you need to think about in your own life. Satan loves when you are following tradition because you are in no way changing anything for the Kingdom of God. Do you follow God or the traditions of man?

Let's wake up today with a shout for our Lord. If people are looking, wake them up!!!

ONE HUNDRED FORTY-FOUR

2 Peter 3:10

But the day of the Lord will come as a thief in the night; in which the heaven will pass away with a great noise, and the elements shall melt with a fervent heat, both the earth and the works that are in it will be burned up.

In Jesus name Amen

The Lord will be returning!! That's because He was here once before!! Oh, what a glorious day that will be!!
He is not coming back silent like a church mouse; He will come with a great noise. Not just any noise, but a GREAT NOISE! Go ahead and praise Him now with a great shout!! We will be loud on the day of His return. Nothing silent going on that day. Practice with a loud praise so you will not be shocked when the rest of us get our praise on for the Lord. Oh, what a glorious day that will be!!

He is coming!
He is coming!
We don't know when but…

HE IS COMING!!!

ONE HUNDRED FORTY-FIVE

Luke 8:15

But the ones that fell on the good ground are those who, having heard the word with noble and good hearts, keep it and bear fruit with patience.

In Jesus name Amen

Patience: waiting without anger and getting upset.

How powerful is your God vs your situation? Patience vs weighing out your facts and wanting things fast. Wait on God! Walk and talk with God and have patience in all your situations!

ONE HUNDRED FORTY-SIX

2 Peter 2:16

But shun profane and idle babbling, for they will increase to more ungodliness.

In Jesus name Amen

Do you live the way God teaches us or do you live as the world? Yes, people make mistakes, just keep trying. God knows your heart and knows that you are trying to live for Him, but God also knows your heart and knows that the worlds way doesn't bother you. You can cuss and swear and are not moved by what you are saying. Or while other people just let words fly out of their mouth and you see nothing wrong with it. The whole world uses words like these little cuss words, so you think...why is it a big deal?

 You better check your heart for God! God says, to shun it, to turn away from it and to keep away from it! You may not understand that person who doesn't like any profanity, but it's not about pleasing you, it's about pleasing God! What God do you serve? The worlds or our mighty Heavenly Father? You will always have a choice.

For me and my house, we will serve and please the Lord, no matter who the world is serving. Check your heart, not the heart of others. Today is the day to choose to follow the Lord and what His word is saying. His hand is always there to help you walk away from ungodliness and if you fall, He is always there to pick you back up.

CHECK YOUR HEART!!

ONE HUNDRED FORTY-SEVEN

Acts 3:6-7

Then Peter said, "Silver and gold I do not have, but what I do have I give you: In the name of Jesus Christ of Nazareth, rise up and walk," And he took him by the right hand and lifted him up, immediately his feet and ankle bones received strength.

In Jesus name Amen

The book of Acts came after Jesus died and rose again. This happened when Jesus took His position beside the Father. Peter, also as a Christian took his position and took the authority that had been given to him and stepped out and did what Jesus said to do. Lay hands on the sick and they will recover!!

Trust Jesus and break man's rules. It's not because of you, it's because of Jesus and His Word and His blood.

Satan does not want this to get in your heart because once there, he can't take it back. He sure can try to lie to you in your mind and say things like this isn't true anymore or this will not work because you are not worthy. It's not about us even though Satan wants us to only focus on ourselves.

It's about Jesus, His word, His blood, and doing His will. Jesus walked this earth to show us how to live and how to walk and what to say. Jesus is coming back, what will you say? Will you blame Him saying that you couldn't follow His Word?

Jesus is with us and with His Word, all things are possible. Just believe, and trust and just have faith! God sees your heart and loves you beyond anything you can imagine!

ONE HUNDRED FORTY-EIGHT

John 3:16

For God so loved the world that He gave His only begotten Son, that whoever believes in Him should not perish but have everlasting life.

In Jesus name Amen

Is there a possibility that one of us here on earth could perish (die and suffer)? Yes, God told us so, but those who BELIEVE in Him and follow His word will not perish but have EVERLASTING (never ending, lasting a long time).

Our life with God will truly never end. We will walk and talk with Him and see and touch Him!! How exciting!!!

Let's not perish but live forever with God! Help someone today to understand this. You don't have to give up your child, just give the Word to someone.

ONE HUNDRED FORTY-NINE

Matthew 6:3-4

But when you do a charitable deed, do not let
your left hand know what your right hand is
doing.
that your charitable deed may be in secret and
your Father who sees in secret will Himself
reward you openly.

In Jesus name Amen

YES AND AMEN!!!!

When you perform charitable deeds, do not
look for gratitude or recognition from man.
God knows your heart and sees that you are
doing good things. Allow your reward to come
from God and do all things unto Him!

ONE HUNDRED FIFTY

Proverbs 24:29

Do not say "I will do to him just as he has done to me; I will render to the man according to his work."

In Jesus name Amen

This is powerful guidance from our Lord. Be forgiving to others. When someone is not kind, show kindness. Don't be like the world. You are the child of the King! Love covers a lot of things you're unaware of. God is using you this day not to pay back evil for evil. Someone is watching to see if you really are the child of the King.

Smile, show love and let God's Spirit shine through you to them. God will take care of evildoers, that isn't your job! You may be part of winning someone's soul back to the Lord and that is more important than getting even. Not an easy thing to do but if the Lord says to do it, then that's what we do!

ONE HUNDRED FIFTY-ONE

Isaiah 28:28-29

Bread flour must be ground, therefore he does not thresh it forever, break it with his cartwheel or crush it with his horseman.
This also comes from the Lord of hosts, who is wonderful in counsel and excellent in guidance.

In Jesus name Amen

Remember in high school, there were counselors, and you would go to them in time of trouble or when you had to make a decision? Today we have the best counselor there is, God! Do you trust God?

He is wonderful and excellent, what more can you ask for? He is waiting, no appointment is needed, and you can talk and listen until your heart is light. Anytime and anywhere! No one on earth can offer you this deal!

God's heart is for you and is the best! Follow Him in all your ways. The road may be rough at times, but that roughness doesn't last. Trust God! He knows the future!

ONE HUNDRED FIFTY-TWO

1 Peter 5:7

Casting all your cares upon Him for He cares for you.

In Jesus name Amen

Casting: Give.
Cares: Anything that bothers you.
Upon: Over.
Him: Jesus.

Give anything that bothers you over to Jesus, He loves you. When you cast something to God, by the time it hits His hand from your heart, it's not the same. He has taken it and turned it around for you.

Picture opening a bubble and speaking the one thing that is really eating at you today into it. Close the bubble and toss it to Jesus. When the bubble lands in the Holy hands of God, the words have now changed. Picture Jesus tossing the bubble back with a smile. Then you open it, and it's empty. All the anxieties, all the burdens and all the worries are now in His hands.

Breathe, what a great day you have before you!!!

ONE HUNDRED FIFTY-THREE

Psalms 27:1-3

The Lord is my light and my salvation; whom shall I fear? The Lord is the strength of my life; whom shall I be afraid?
When the wicked come against me to eat up my flesh, my enemies and foes, they stumbled and fell
Though an army may encamp against me, my heart shall not fear; Though war may rise against me, in this I will be confident.

In Jesus name Amen

The Lord is your strength! Have confidence in Him! Step out in faith in the Lord and His strength! Your enemy will stumble and fall!

Build your foundation on God's Word and when trouble hits, know He is not a God who lies or uses empty words. Stand strong, stand tall, and know that your enemy will stumble and fall as God says. You are not alone!!

Satan can yell loud and stomp his feet and even roar like a lion, but remember, he may roar LIKE a lion, but he is NOT THE LION!!! Our God is the Lion of Judah. Satan runs when he sees the real Lion.

Whom shall we fear? NO ONE!! Rejoice in the Lord!

ONE HUNDRED FIFTY-FOUR

2 Peter 2:8

But, beloved do not forget this one thing that with the Lord one day is as 1000 years and 1000 years as one day.

In Jesus name Amen

Here is something to think about: God's thoughts are so much bigger than ours. Can we trust and put faith in Him? YES, I want His thoughts guiding me because He will take me higher than I can even think about for myself.

We honor only You this high, our Lord Jesus!

We close our eyes and see you giving us hugs. Father, we return your hugs with honor for loving us so much!

ONE HUNDRED FIFTY-FIVE

1 Peter 3:10-12

He who loves life and sees good days, let him refrain his tongue from evil, and his lips from speaking deceit.
let him turn away from evil and do good, let him speak peace and pursue it.
for the eyes of the Lord are on the righteous and His ears are open to their prayers; but the face of the Lord is against those who do evil.

In Jesus name Amen

Another insight from the Lord is, He tells us how to get His attention. His eyes and His ears are open to OUR PRAYERS.

When people push your buttons, hold Jesus' hand, look into His eyes, and do right in all your ways.

SEEK PEACE.

PURSUE IT.

HOLD YOUR TONGUE.

His ears are open to your prayers! Lord, give us spiritual ears to hear what your Spirit is saying!

ONE HUNDRED FIFTY-SIX

Colossians 2:15

Having disarmed principalities and power, he made a public spectacle of them, triumphing over them in it.

In Jesus name Amen

Remember the verse that says NO WEAPON formed against you shall prosper? This verse explains why!!! Jesus disarms our enemies down into hell. When Jesus was on the cross, Satan thought he had killed Jesus forever. Then when Satan went home and looked over his shoulder, there stood Jesus! Jesus was the only one qualified who had no sin to go get the keys back from Satan, the one who stole them in the first place. Jesus also took power away from the demons.

Satan can put a carrot in front of you, then you make the choice to take it or not. When you have decisions to make, always take them to the Lord. When Satan has a battle against you and you feel weary, stand strong. Jesus took the victory and gave it to His children, you and I. Aren't you glad you're his child?

We will not be defeated!! NEVER!!

Satan, who is a bully, acts so big and bad, but Jesus stripped him! Satan has no power over God's children!!

ONE HUNDRED FIFTY-SEVEN

Mark 4:23

If anyone has ears to hear, let him hear.

In Jesus name Amen

In many Bible verses, Jesus tells us this and says, "if anyone has ears let him hear" what the Spirit is saying. You do have the ability to hear the Holy Spirit. You must tune in by reading the Word and listening.

Seek the Lord while He is near! Close the world out and hear what the Spirit is saying to you! Humble yourself unto Him. It is the most treasured time, EVER!! Anywhere and anytime! Listen with spiritual ears.

Are you born again? If not, when you are, you get new ears. Spiritual ones!

Whatever comes from God is good and the best!!

ONE HUNDRED FIFTY-EIGHT

1 John 5:4

For whatever is born of God overcomes the world. And this is the victory that has overcome the world - our faith.

In Jesus name Amen

How do you get victory in what you are going through? Faith in your Lord!!

No matter what you're going through, you already have the victory!! God has a plan, and your faith makes the plan come alive. With your faith, you can move forward as He hands the victory to you! We have the answer before we even ask the question! Before you ask, "how long will it take?" Read Job! Job kept the faith in the Lord, even without knowing the answer!

Don't stop! Move forward! Why would you stop? You have already been given the papers with VICTORY stamped all over them. Victory over the world and everything in it!

We are His children. We have His word to stand on! We stand on a foundation that does not sink! Head up, stand tall with your faith and move forward!
Keep living by God's Word and you win!!!

ONE HUNDRED FIFTY-NINE

Galatians 6:9

Let us not grow weary while doing good, for in due season we shall reap if we do not lose heart.

In Jesus name Amen

Check your heart, does it beat for God? Don't let a situation change your heart for the Lord. Ask yourself, what am I looking at the most? The Word of God or my situation? Live by what God's Words say. Your situation is trying to overcome you and tell you it is too much. Take your eyes off the situation and pray and seek God. Don't let Satan steal your heartbeat for God. Don't hand over your heart to Satan. God tells you, in due season, if you don't lose heart. That means yes, He is watching, He sees, and He hears. Does He hear your heart beating for Him? Does He see your heart beating for Him? If you grow weary, you have given up your season to Satan.

If you fall, just get back up! Jump start your heart with God's Words. Let your heart beat loud and hard for God. God wants your situation, let Him take it from you. Focus on God's Word, not all the stuff around you. While you continue to walk by faith, let God work on your situation.

ONE HUNDRED SIXTY

Matthew 11:28

Come to me all you who labor and are heavy laden and I will give you rest.

In Jesus name Amen

You must come! When things are bothering you, how far do you go on your own before you go to the Lord? Call His name, He is always right there! Your Lord has the answer. He knows you will labor on your own and have a heavy heart. He says come to Him! Only He can give you true rest.

God tells us: "come as you are." That means to come however you are able with a heart calling to Him. You must take the first step and come to Him, and He will answer. He is a gentleman and will not force you. You have free will. God does not lie, He said…when you come, I will give you rest. Open your heart and speak to your Lord, Jesus Christ!

ONE HUNDRED SIXTY-ONE

Proverbs 19:17

He who has pity on the poor lends to the Lord, and He will pay back what he has given.

In Jesus name Amen

He, the Lord will pay you back. The Lord sees how you help others and how you give. You cannot outgive the Lord! Give with a joyful heart in all your giving! Never be afraid of helping someone, even when you know they can't pay you back.

God has your back!

God's Word is, YES and AMEN!

ONE HUNDRED SIXTY-TWO

Romans 10:13

For whoever calls on the name of the Lord shall be saved.

In Jesus name Amen

"Whoever." Are you whoever? Yes! Don't look at your past, it has nothing to do with the Lord accepting you. His love for you sees nothing from the past when you call on Him and ask for forgiveness.

Yes! Call on Him today, It's that easy!! Jesus is waiting with open loving arms!!

There is no secret formula, just call on the Lord with a true heart!!

ONE HUNDRED SIXTY-THREE

2 Corinthians 3:6

For it was God who commanded light to shine out of the darkness, who has shone in our hearts to give the light of the knowledge of the glory of God in the face of Jesus Christ.

In Jesus name Amen

The light in your heart was freely given to you. Now freely give it to the world, the dark place.

ONE HUNDRED SIXTY-FOUR

Titus 2:11-12

For the grace of God that brings salvation has appeared to all men.
teaching us that, denying ungodliness and worldly lusts, we should live soberly, righteously, and godly in the present age.

In Jesus name Amen

Let's not point fingers at sin but let's not call sin okay, either. Just because the world has decided that it's not sin and voted that something is okay, does not mean that God has approved.

Call sin what it is but ask God to help us share His Word in order to change a life. Pointing a finger does no good but helping to change someone's life is a great service to God.

Don't give up, keep sharing, smiling, and feeding people the love of God. We all need God. His Word does not leave us empty!

ONE HUNDRED SIXTY-FIVE

Titus 3:9

But avoid foolish disputes, genealogies, contentions, and strivings about the law; for they are unprofitable and useless.

In Jesus name Amen

Disputes: To argue about something.
Contentions: heated disagreements.
Striving: to struggle or fight forcefully.
Foolish: lacking good sense or judgement; unwise.

Weigh out all things that you think you should stand your ground on. Some things in life are a waste of time. To spend a lot of time on these things is useless.

ONE HUNDRED SIXTY-SIX

2 Timothy 4:2

Preach the word! Be ready in season and out of season. Convince, rebuke, exhort, with all long suffering and teaching.

In Jesus name Amen

Be ready every day for your Lord. Be ready in any season! Always be ready to spread His Word, for we know not when our Lord will appear!

ONE HUNDRED SIXTY-SEVEN

Matthew 5:9

Blessed are the peace makers for they shall be called sons of God.

In Jesus name Amen

Such a short but powerful Word from God. Do you want to be right, or do you want to be sons of God? Do you want to honor the flesh, or do you want to follow the will of God?

Be blessed today and be the peacemaker. Don't let your flesh overrule the Word of God. Sons of God, stand strong and show your loving light!!

ONE HUNDRED SIXTY-EIGHT

1 Peter 2:9-10

But you are a chosen generation, a royal priesthood, a Holy nation, His own special people, that you may proclaim the praises of Him who called you out of darkness and into marvelous light
who once were not a people but are now the people of God, who had not obtained mercy but have obtained mercy.

In Jesus name Amen

Let's pray for people more than ever! Let's ask people to come and share God's Word with us at church. That person that is like sandpaper to you, that person that never speaks to you, that person who demands attention whether good or bad, that person who says the meanest things, God desires them like He desires you. It took time for you to turn to God and it will take time for them also. You may need to speak first, give first, turn your cheek first, and come back another day with more loving words from God.

To God they are worth it!! We are here to do God's work, not our own!

ONE HUNDRED SIXTY-NINE

Philippians 2:11

That every tongue should confess that Jesus Christ is Lord, to be glory of God the Father.

In Jesus name Amen

Go ahead and boldly be a witness for the Lord. If they don't accept the Word of the Lord, and you have done it in a kind way, just move on. They are rejecting the Almighty God, not you personally. One day, maybe not today, they will confess that Jesus Christ is Lord and Jesus will tell them that He had sent you on that special day for you to witness to them.

Stand strong, move with a smile and always be a light in the darkness. Don't let the world have a strong hold on your days of being a witness unto the Lord!

ONE HUNDRED SEVENTY

2 Corinthians 9:6

But this I say: he who sows sparingly will also reap sparingly, and he who sows bountifully will also reap bountifully.

In Jesus name Amen

Be a cheerful giver, be happy in your heart and give it freely. God does bless a heart that gives freely. If you only give because you feel like you have to, you are better off keeping it in your pocket.

If someone is doing wrong with the things that are given to them, it's God's job to deal with them, not yours.

You are told by God to be a giver but it's not always money. It's money, time, clothes, gifts, tithing and so on. Let your heart be happy in your giving. Do not give only to get something in return or to show off, give with a cheerful heart and because you want to please God!

ONE HUNDRED SEVENTY-ONE

Ephesians 4:5-6

There is one Lord one faith one baptism.
one God and one Father of all, who is above all,
and through all, and in you all.

In Jesus name Amen

It is a relationship with God, not a religion with
God. How many religions are there? Why?

Follow the one God with a relationship, not as a
man with a religion.

ONE HUNDRED SEVENTY-TWO

John 3:20-21

For everyone practicing evil hates the light and does not come to the light, lest deeds should be exposed.
he is the truth comes to light that his deed may be clearly see that they have been done in God.

In Jesus name Amen

When you do things for people, do it unto the Lord. If the Lord puts a light on your deeds, will you be ashamed or will you be like a child smiling knowing your Heavenly Father is so proud of you?

God knows your heart. Do everything in the name of Jesus. Always let God be the one who puts a light on what your deeds are, not you!

ONE HUNDRED SEVENTY-THREE

John 4:24

God is a spirit, and those who worship Him must worship in spirit and in truth.

In Jesus name Amen

Worship: Honor.

Let's honor our Lord today! In Spirit, a Spirit that is alive!! Yes, there are many ways to worship our Lord. Try a new way and honor God with an exciting heart!! Let's build a real relationship with God. Love on God today! He is already loving on you right now!!

ONE HUNDRED SEVENTY-FOUR

Philippians 4:8

Finally brother, whatever things are true, whatever things are noble, whatever things are just, whatever things are pure, whatever things are lovely, whatever things are of good report, if there is any virtue and if there is anything praiseworthy – meditate on these things.

In Jesus name Amen

Don't let your mind run crazy! Don't let this area which is the battleground tell you how your day is going to be! Replace your thoughts with what this verse is saying. Start out with praise to the Lord and all the good can replace what Satan is trying to make bad. Choose these thoughts today and have a great day!!

God's Words can change your whole day!

ONE HUNDRED SEVENTY-FIVE

1 Timothy 3:16

God was manifested in the flesh, justified in the Spirit, seen by Angels, preached among the Gentiles, believed on in the world, and received up in Glory.

In Jesus name Amen

Jesus did all of this for you!!

Your Jesus! Your healer! Your joy! Your provider! Your helper! Your everything! Just for you!

Need to talk? He is waiting! Start your day with a blessing and smile.

Our Lord is!!!

ONE HUNDRED SEVENTY-SIX

Proverbs 17:22

A merry heart does good like medicine: but a broken spirit dries the bones.

In Jesus name Amen

How do you get a merry heart? Think of happy times, think of your children, think of your grandchildren.

Sing a song unto the Lord. When you're sad and down and can't stop thinking of what you are going through, you make Satan happy because you are handing over your joy to him. He dries your bones, and you feel like you can't move.

Stand up, look up and take your medicine daily with the Lord! You can change your day with the Lord!

My Lord is my medicine! What is yours?

ONE HUNDRED SEVENTY-SEVEN

Psalms 100:1, 2, 4

Make a joyful shout to the Lord, all you lands!
Serve the Lord with gladness, come before His
presence with singing.
Enter His gates with thanksgiving and into His
courts with praise.

In Jesus name Amen

We have the key to open the door. With the
Bible telling us so many times to make a joyful
shout and sing, it gives you strength to make it
through a day that you didn't think you could
get through.

If you have never walked by faith in this part of
your praise, then it's time to give a sacrifice of
praise. You don't have to give your life; Jesus
has already walked that path for you. He is
worthy of your praise, and He tells us how to
give it. It is so refreshing to praise our Lord in
so many ways.

Your enemy, Satan does not want you to get
this. Did you know in the Old Testament they
put the praise and worship team in front of the
army as the men marched out to war? Do you
have

something you are fighting? Start with a song and a shout and watch your strength grow.

ONE HUNDRED SEVENTY-EIGHT

Mark 16:19-20

So then after the Lord had spoken unto them, he was received up into Heaven and sat on the right hand of God.
And they went forth, and preached everywhere, the Lord working with them. And confirming the Word with signs following.

In Jesus name Amen

Jesus sat down because His work was done. Now it's our turn. He tells us to do what He did on earth.

What did He do?

He preached the Fathers Word everywhere He went. He laid hands on everyday people and healed them, and signs followed Him.

It is what God is telling us to do. Step out and say, speak, and share God's Word. Keep faith in the words you speak, which are God's Words, not yours. God will do what He tells us he will do. God will heal. God will make the signs follow. Your work is to lay hands on the sick, the rest is God's. They will recover!

Be obedient to His word! Do your part and God always stays true to His promises. You may not see it right away, but it will happen!

ONE HUNDRED SEVENTY-NINE

1 Corinthians 2:9

But as it is written: Eye has not seen, nor ear heard, nor have entered into the heart of man the things which God has prepared for those who love Him.

In Jesus name Amen

How much does God love you? He sent His son to die for you! Before you were born, the Lord knew you. That means He saw you; He knew your name before your mom did. He knew what you would like and dislike and His love goes on and on!! He prepared something for you, which means He waits for your coming. He has something just for you! Your human mind cannot imagine what your Lord has prepared for you. When you have this kind of love flowing from the throne of God, He watches you every day. He knows what you are going through, and He is guiding you and holding your hand. Your God only has good things for you!

When it looks like Satan has the upper hand and he is whispering lies to you, remember he is the biggest liar there is. If you know someone who lies a lot, do you listen to them? You give no time or energy to the lies they speak. So do the same with Satan! Yes, you have authority over him! Tell Satan who you are in Christ Jesus and keep your eyes on what God is saying.

Your Father's eyes are always on you and His ears are always hearing and listening to you, His child! Yes, you are a beloved child of the Almighty God, and He has already prepared a way out of your situation. Your Father, your God, is always with you!

That's true love!!

ONE HUNDRED EIGHTY

1 Corinthians 2:14

But the natural man do not receive the things of the Spirit of God, for they are foolishness to him; nor can he know them, because they are spiritually discerned.

In Jesus name Amen

Jesus has told us about many things in His Word. Do you believe some of them or all of them?

Yes, you are different from the world. You belong to another world that is truer than the world you live in. When you know Him and love Him and are born again, it all begins to come together as you read His word. Don't get too mad at the world that thinks Jesus is a joke and God is too old fashioned. Their thinking just shows you what world they belong to. Show them Jesus by the way you live and speak. They are blinded to the truth right now, help them see the light and they too will come to know Jesus. They will realize how foolish the world is without Jesus. Don't condemn them but love them into wisdom!

ONE HUNDRED EIGHTY-ONE

Proverbs 3:5-6

Trust in the Lord with all your heart and lean
not on your own understanding.
In all your way acknowledge Him, and He shall
direct your paths.

In Jesus name Amen

Dear Father,

I do not have to understand, I trust you with
my every breath. I know that you are a good
Father and that you take my hand and lead me,
just like I did with my little child. I know your
love is so much deeper than my heart
understands. I stand before you God and say,
THANK YOU! I trust you!

ONE HUNDRED EIGHTY-TWO

Ephesians 5:1

Therefore, be imitators of God as dear little children.

In Jesus name Amen

Some of us are just little babies in the Lord even though we are in our adult human years, but as you grow you will want to be more and more like what God instructs you to be. Keep renewing your mind with the Word of the Lord and also be a doer. Imitating means doing something. As a child of God this is where you let your light shine in the darkness of the world.

Dear Father,

I come to the throne boldly to say THANK YOU for being my God and for being a doer of Your Word always! I trust you with everything! Father, help me be more like You in every situation. As I grow, I THANK YOU for showing me how to grow in You.

ONE HUNDRED EIGHTY-THREE

2 Corinthians 5:7

For we walk by faith, and not by sight.

In Jesus name Amen

Such a short, but extremely powerful verse!

If you're in a situation that doesn't look or feel good, close your eyes and by faith see your situation the way God does! When you close your eyes, you have closed the doors on Satan. Satan walks by sight. He puts you through things to make you feel and see and to try and force you to not have faith.

We don't have to see how things are going to change, by faith we already know they will! Open the Bible and read your Father's Word out loud. Build your faith muscles!! Walk by faith and not by sight! Praise God in the storm because the storm must go! Look up and know that your God is faithful!!

ONE HUNDRED EIGHTY-FOUR

Psalms 147:1

For it is good to sing to our God; For it is pleasant, and praise is beautiful.

In Jesus name Amen

The Lord says, IT IS GOOD TO SING! It is pleasant to our Lord and God says it is beautiful!

Let's give God what He is worthy of. In knowing our God and giving Him praise, it sets our day on the right foot. So, SING every chance you get today!! God smiles upon you and the Holy Spirit will be jumping for joy inside you!

Sing loud, sing with love, sing unto the Lord today!

ONE HUNDRED EIGHTY-FIVE

Proverbs 8:32

Now therefore, listen to me my children, for blessed are those who keep my ways.

In Jesus name Amen

Keep the Lord's way, not what your friends and others are doing. Not what the workplace is doing. Not what your neighbors are doing. Not what the world is doing. If you are currently doing things because of anyone but God, turn away from it and run back to the Lord. When the Lord says you will be blessed if you do it His way, LOOK OUT, the blessings will overtake you! Do good while you wait upon the Lord!

ONE HUNDRED EIGHTY-SIX

James 3:14-16

But if you have bitter envy and self-seeking in your hearts, do not boast and lie against the truth.
this wisdom does not descend from above, but earthly, sensual demonic
for where envy and self-seeking exist, confusion and every evil thing there are.

In Jesus name Amen

Choose to devote yourself fully to God rather than to your own selfish and worldly desires. Devote yourself to the Lord, and Godly wisdom and righteousness will begin to grow in your life.

One step at a time!

ONE HUNDRED EIGHTY-SEVEN

James 5:13

Is anyone among you suffering? Let him pray, is anyone cheerful? Let him sing psalms.

In Jesus name Amen

Find a good church where you can be yourself and be honest. When you do, they will not judge you or put you in a certain group. God wants us to be able to share when our hearts hurt and wants us to be our true selves. Share your heart when it's sad or when you are going through hard times. Sing with others when your heart is singing. Let's learn to lift people up with support. Support with the Lord's Word and with Love!

ONE HUNDRED EIGHTY-EIGHT

2 Corinthians 10:5

Casting down arguments and every high thing that exalts itself against the knowledge of God, bring every thought into captivity to the obedience of Christ.

In Jesus name Amen

I come before you my Father, I bow before you. You are my King; you are my Lord! Thank you for showing me this word today. I needed to be reminded that these small arguments are just trying to hold me back from being the best I can be. I need to hold my tongue and share your love, not give a piece of my mind. I will take these thoughts and cast them down. I will walk more in peace and love. Forgive me for grieving the Holy Spirit. I LOVE YOU, GOD!

ONE HUNDRED EIGHTY-NINE

1 Corinthians 13:11

When I was a child, I spoke as a child, I understood as a child, I thought as a child; but when I became a man, I put away childish things.

In Jesus name Amen

Grow up and take responsibility as an adult. There is a certain time and place for things. As a man/woman we must be responsible for all we do and play no blame games. Don't be childish, silly and immature. Be childlike with good qualities such as innocence and being trustworthy. God wants us to be childlike with Him. Trust Him always, just as a child looks up to and trusts their parents to protect and love them!

ONE HUNDRED NINETY

Matthew 16:19

And I will give you the keys of the kingdom of heaven and whatever you bind on earth will be bound in heaven, and whatever you loose on earth will be loosed in heaven.

In Jesus name Amen

Jesus has given us authority (the keys). We have authority over sin! Bind this habit that is not from God. Yes, we do have power over things here on earth. Why was the authority given? In the spirit world, you speak to it and bind it and it is done in Heaven!! Keep the Word close to your heart and mouth. Any thought that comes and it is not from God, I bind the thought in the name of Jesus and I loose good thought on that subject. I will not jump every time Satan tells me to be afraid, hate or, anything else. If it is not from God, it does not receive my energy. It is time to take your position in the Kingdom of God, a position of authority!!

ONE HUNDRED NINETY-ONE

Ephesians 2:10

For we are His workmanship, created in Christ
Jesus for good works, which God prepared
beforehand that we should walk in them.

In Jesus name Amen

God is the God that shall not lie. You were
made by God, picked by God, and made special
by God. You were made for good works. Let's
get out there in the world and do His good
works. Shine, forgive, love, and put on the true
you! This is the reason God made you! You
were made by God for God. Let's walk it out
today in honor of our living God!

ONE HUNDRED NINETY-TWO

Mark 11:22

So, Jesus answered and said to them, "Have faith in God."

In Jesus name Amen

Faith: believing what God says is true before you see it.

In our heads, we want to see things happen (proof), then rejoice that it happened. God says, with faith, believe without seeing it and rejoice before you see it. Remember, it is God and not man that we put our faith in. Man will let you down! We walk by faith and not by sight. God hears His children and God is never late! Step out today in your heart and ask God, then believe He has already given it to you. God does not work by time, He holds time. Have faith in our God and wait while rejoicing in the Lord.

ONE HUNDRED NINETY-THREE

Philippians 4:19

And my God will supply every need of yours according to his riches in glory in Christ Jesus.

In Jesus name Amen

You have needs living here on Earth and God knows your needs. Have a one-on-one conversation with your Heavenly Father about what you need. Then thank Him for meeting those needs. God said He will meet every need you have. Trust Your Father by Faith.

Things are getting crazy out there but there is no need for us to follow the craziness with the Holy Spirit living inside of us. Relax and know that God will meet every need for you and give you wisdom during this time.

ONE HUNDRED NINETY-FOUR

James 1:5-6

If any of you lacks wisdom, let him ask God,
who gives generously to all without reproach,
and it will be given him.
But let him ask in faith, with no doubting, for
the one who doubts is like a wave of the sea
that is driven and tossed by the wind.

In Jesus name Amen

You may start out in DOUBT, I recommend
finding that one verse that talks you through
your situation. Let your own ears hear your own
voice say the Words of God so it drops deep
into your heart. The Word of God will raise up
in your heart and all doubt will turn into big
time faith! Never give up and always ask God
for HIS wisdom in your situation. God will
never leave you and will help you grow as you
draw close to Him. After life with God's Word,
you will find you are no longer like a wave that
is driven and tossed by the sea. You will find
your foundation is stronger and stronger in
Faith without doubt. You aren't born and then
you go to college the next week. With God, you
are born again, and you walk with Him and
your faith grows!

Never feel guilty about doubt, just don't give up. Satan gives guilt to you to make you give up. Know that you learn as you go with God and your doubting disappears!

You are the apple of God's eye!!! Keep growing with and in the Lord and doubt will be a thing of the past. It will be YES and AMEN to all of God's Words that you have stored deep in your heart.

ONE HUNDRED NINETY-FIVE

Romans 12:19

Beloved, never avenge yourselves, but leave it to the wrath of God, for it is written, "Vengeance is mine, I will repay, says the Lord."

In Jesus name Amen

Love your enemies. Yes, this is backward from our thinking. Who is smarter you or God? Never repay the people who hurt you. They may think they are a jump ahead of you, but guess what? God is smarter than they are!!! God is not a God who lies! "Vengeance is mine, I will repay", says the Lord. God has your back. You keep walking up-right and smile. God feels your heart and He will make things right for you.

ONE HUNDRED NINETY-SIX

James 3:10

Out of the same mouth come praise and cursing. My brothers and sisters, this should not be.

In Jesus name Amen

I felt led by the Holy Spirit to bring it back so that it is at the center of our attention. So, I hope we all take notice as to what SHOULD come out of our mouth and what should NOT. The words: "this should not be" really gets my attention!

ONE HUNDRED NINETY-SEVEN

2 Timothy 4:2

Preach the word; be instant in season, out of season; reprove, rebuke, exhort with all longsuffering and doctrine.

In Jesus name Amen

No excuses! You see people, there is your chance! Do it for your Jesus. Jesus loves them all. Let's go tell them just that! Jesus loves you!

ONE HUNDRED NINETY-EIGHT

Psalm 150:1-6

Praise the Lord! Praise God in His sanctuary;
Praise Him in his mighty heavens!
Praise Him for His mighty deeds; Praise Him
according to His excellent greatness!
Praise Him with trumpet sound; Praise Him
with lute and harp!
Praise Him with tambourine and dance; Praise
Him with strings and pipe!
Praise Him with sounding cymbals; Praise Him
with loud clashing cymbals!
Let everything that has breath praise the Lord.

In Jesus name Amen

Praising the Lord Jesus Christ is an honor! Our
mighty God deserves all our praise. It's not
entertainment, it's a true straight from the
heart praise! Sing, shout, dance, jump and do it
with the instruments. It's for God one hundred
percent! Just remember, when you see this kind
of praise, it's for God who loves it!! It has
nothing to do with your liking it or not. God is
worthy of all our praises! How can we not get
excited about praising our Lord Jesus Christ
who gave us so much?!

ONE HUNDRED NINETY-NINE

1 Peter 5:7

Casting all your anxieties on Him, because He cares for you.

In Jesus name Amen

We are in times where it seems so easy to fall into anxiety. Stress and fear are real. Remember to truly lean on the Lord and share your feelings with Him and don't forget to also leave it in His hands. Because He cares for you, He will turn your anxiety into peace. Don't look too far into the future and give it a place to drive you crazy. That is not of God! Take each day and hand over the anxiety and fears to your Father, right at the moment they hit you, who will turn things around for you. The Almighty has good reasons to tell you to "CAST ALL YOUR ANXIETY ON HIM." Be a good child and just listen to your Heavenly Father. In the long run, letting God have it ALL makes a better life for you.

TWO HUNDRED

Luke 15:7

I tell you, there will be more joy in heaven over one sinner who repents than over ninety-nine righteous persons who need no repentance.

In Jesus name Amen

See how much God loves you! Joy is in "HEAVEN" because of "YOU" every time you truly repent!

TWO HUNDRED ONE

Psalms 46:10

Be still and know that I am God; I will be exalted among the nations, I will be exalted in the earth.

In Jesus name Amen

Oh, exalted our God!! Place God highly in our lives above everything! Then JUST be still from your busy life and find a private place that you can go into and be still. Just see God is there with you and be still. Oh, how beautiful His whispers are! Yes, He whispers just to you. Be still, be quiet and listen to that one and only voice, God!!!!! He is talking to you because He loves you. Are you listening?

TWO HUNDRED TWO

Romans 8:5

For those who live according to the flesh set their minds on the things of the flesh, but those who live according to the Spirit set their minds on the things of the Spirit.

In Jesus name Amen

Always do your best to live by the Bible. Doing things your way will always end with crazy living and you will always ask "Why is this happening to me?" It's because you follow your flesh and you're doing things your way instead of God's way. Trust your God to guide you and then do things His way. Keep your mind on our Lord Jesus Christ and see all the things change to great things for you! He loves you and tells you things for YOU to be blessed. Think about it.

TWO HUNDRED THREE

Matthew 5:4

Blessed are those who mourn, for they will be comforted.

In Jesus name Amen

No matter what you're mourning, God said He will comfort you. He will!! Stay close to God and don't pull away from Him. This is the time He is holding you! Sometimes in our mourning, we can't feel Him because we are not feeling anything. God is there and He is holding you. It is God who knows how to truly comfort you. In your private place, get in His lap and be comforted. He loves you so much! We don't have to understand, just trust Your Jesus Christ.

TWO HUNDRED FOUR

Mark 16:17-18

And these signs will follow those who believe:
In My name they will cast out demons; they will
speak with new tongues.
they will take up serpents; and if they drink
anything deadly, it will by no means hurt them;
they will lay hands on the sick, and they will
recover.

In Jesus name Amen

See Jesus already did everything on the cross
for us and a trip to Hell to take the authority
away from Satan that Adam and Eve gave to
him. Now, since Jesus did it all, what do you
need to do? You must believe what He did for
you. Believe you now have the authority over all
evil!! Believe you can lay hands on the sick and
they will recover. Don't fear Satan, let Satan
fear you because you BELIEVE in the Almighty
Jesus Christ and all that He did for you!
Believe... Be a doer... Once this falls from your
head into your heart, you will no longer let
Satan be the dictator in your life. Jesus now
rules in your life! Satan will now fear YOU!!!
FEAR NOT!

TWO HUNDRED FIVE

James 4:8

Draw near to God and He will draw near to you.
Cleanse your hands, you sinners; and purify
your hearts, you double-minded.

In Jesus name Amen

You are as close to God as you want to be. Get
born again and ask for forgiveness of your sins
and invite Jesus inside your heart and to be the
Lord of your life! You're more than halfway
there! Now, read more and more and hear more
and more about who Jesus is. Your doubts will
disappear, and you will only do things God's
way and that cleans your hands. Your heart is
now purified with the Holy Spirit living inside
you. You now have a relationship with Jesus.
It's not just a religious thing. Some people are
just religious and happy with that and stop
right there! But others choose to draw closer to
Jesus and have a true relationship with Him!!
Which one do you want? Jesus loves you so
much He wants a relationship with you. Jesus is
a gentleman and will wait on you. Now is
always a good time to start.

TWO HUNDRED SIX

James 4:7

Submit yourselves, then, to God. Resist the devil, and he will flee from you.

In Jesus name Amen

Did you know Satan is a squatter? Satan is trespassing when he tries to put you down, he tells you that you are no good! Satan is trying to set up camp in your head! Your body is the temple of God and the Holy Spirit lives in you if you are born again! If someone came onto your land to set up camp and then yell bad things out at you, you would take authority and kick him off your land!! No second thoughts about it! Don't sit and listen to this squatter who is trying to set up camp in your head! KICK HIM OUT! DON'T GIVE HIM A SECOND THOUGHT!!! JUST DO IT!!! He is a pushy someone and all you have to do is push him back! Resist Him with the sword. And you know the sword is God's word. Satan must flee when you stand on God's Word. Nothing is more powerful! Now get back to who paid the price for you and listen to that voice and hear what He is saying about you!

TWO HUNDRED SEVEN

John 3:16

For God so loved the world that he gave his one and only Son, that whoever believes in him shall not perish but have eternal life.

In Jesus name Amen

His one and only Son! His one and only Beloved Son! His one and only Sinless Son! His one and only Well Pleasing Son! His one and only Obedient Son! It was all for US! To make us His children!

Some hate Him! Some cuss Him! Some deny Him! Some laugh at Him! Some walk away from Him! Some mock Him! Some doubt Him! Some put Him last! Some lie about Him! Yes, He sent His son to die for ALL of US, even when He knew some people would do all the above things.

How much does God love you? Just think about your life and know no matter what you have done, God knew it and still sent His Son. His Son Jesus Christ knew it and still agreed with His Father to come. How much does God really love us? Can we even count the ways? If you chose Jesus Christ today, you too could have internal life!

TWO HUNDRED EIGHT

1 John 1:9

If we confess our sins, he is faithful and just to forgive us our sins and to cleanse us from all unrighteousness.

In Jesus name Amen

How are you doing on forgiveness toward others? It's about God's way, not your way. It's funny how we expect God to forgive us so quickly but when it's our turn to pass this love on to others, it's like we can accept being forgiven but we are not able to be the "forgiver." We want to say: "yeah but," "yeah but." I am so glad Jesus Christ didn't say that. Pride sure can stand and block YOUR blessing, not THEIRS. Is it truly worth giving up your blessing to hold on to that bitterness?

TWO HUNDRED NINE

Ephesians 4:2

Be completely humble and gentle; be patient, bearing with one another in love.

In Jesus name Amen

God said it! We can do it! Never give up! Always work toward the mark!!!!

TWO HUNDRED TEN

James 4:17

So whoever knows the right thing to do and fails to do it, for him it is sin.

In Jesus name Amen

Always be honest with yourself. Others may not know what you know, but God does. You can't deceive God. You know God's Word so always do what is right with God, not what you can get away with. If you take things without permission, you have failed to do what is right. You have sinned. Love God so much that you want to do right.

TWO HUNDRED ELEVEN

James1:13

When tempted, no one should say, "God is tempting me." For God cannot be tempted by evil, nor does he tempt anyone; but each person is tempted when they are dragged away by their own evil desire and enticed. Then, after desire has conceived, it gives birth to sin; and sin, when it is full-grown, gives birth to death.

In Jesus name Amen

Your temptation starts as a thought and if you don't replace that bad thought with God's Word, you have opened the door for Satan to build on that thought and your temptation is now living, and a decision will be made. If you don't replace those sinful thoughts with God's Word, you have opened that door and entered into an action that you are now giving birth to. This sin will bring death to you starting in your heart after the act has taken place. Not only does it affect you but the loved ones around you. God does not tempt you. God has told you to choose life. Jesus and His ways are life to you, to your heart and to your loved ones. Cast down any bad thoughts right away! It's not worth giving birth to any evil things in your life.

TWO HUNDRED TWELVE

Psalm 65:1

Praise awaits you, O God, in Zion; to you our vows will be fulfilled. O you who hear prayer, to you all men will come. When we were overwhelmed by sins, you forgave our transgressions. Blessed are those you choose and bring near to live in your courts!

In Jesus name Amen

Start this day while we have Mercy and Grace to draw closer to the one who gave His life for YOU! His name is Jesus Christ. Don't let Satan lie to you, that you cannot come before Jesus Christ because of your dirty sins, that are glued to you forever! When you ask for forgiveness and turn away from that sin, you have been washed by the blood of Jesus Christ and He sees you as white as snow. Stand up with authority that you are what God calls you!! White as snow with no sin in sight! Praise His Name for the great love that He has for You and has shown you by His action. Wake up with praise in your mouth!

TWO HUNDRED THIRTEEN

Matthew 7:7

Ask and it will be given to you; seek and you will find; knock and the door will be opened to you.

In Jesus name Amen

You must act on God's Word first. Jesus acted on your behalf first, He gave His life over for your sins. Now YOU must do something first. YOU must ASK, then you will receive. YOU must SEEK, then you will find. YOU must KNOCK, and it will be open to you. Today is the day! Now is the time! Ask by FAITH. Seek by FAITH. Knock by FAITH. You can't have faith one day, then unbelief the next. That is, you believe God one day then believe Satan the next! You cannot serve two Father's.

TWO HUNDRED FOURTEEN

Matthew 6:25

Do Not Worry "Therefore I tell you, do not worry about your life, what you will eat or drink; or about your body, what you will wear. Is not life more than food, and the body more than clothes?

In Jesus name Amen

God says: do not worry!! So, sing or hook this song up on your phone and sing your worries away. When you have a moment that comes all over you to worry. Just sing:

Hakuna Matata (It means NO WORRIES). Then your heart and spirit feel better and now Satan is the one concerned with why you aren't consumed with all the worry he just thought he gave you. We have the VICTORY!!! Now trust your Lord Jesus Christ with a great and full heart. He has gotten you through other things and He will again! Hallelujah!

TWO HUNDRED FIFTEEN

James 4:2

You desire but do not have, so you kill. You covet but you cannot get what you want, so you quarrel and fight. You do not have, because you do not ask God.

In Jesus name Amen

If you're not asking God for it, then you know you should not wonder in your mind.

TWO HUNDRED SIXTEEN

James 4:14

Whereas you do not know what will happen tomorrow. For what is your life? It is even a vapor that appears for a little time and then vanishes away.

In Jesus name Amen

Our lives only last for a little while on Earth. Heaven is for always! Plan your future place in a forever place. It's the place to be!!! Hell is not a place you want to plan to go. Torture is for infinity. Heaven is a celebration forever!!! It's not God's decision, it's your decision. Let's help others get to the celebration for life.

TWO HUNDRED SEVENTEEN

Proverbs 10:25

As the whirlwind passeth, so is the wicked no more: but the righteous is an everlasting foundation.

In Jesus name Amen

Stand right with God! Don't size things up by the way a man lives. The everlasting foundation is what I've been talking about all week. You may think: what do I need to do to change for this new life? Nothing, after you ask God into your heart and start reading His Word you will find that your heart is a new heart, and you will want to do things differently. We are all still learning God's way and growing into what is truly best for us. As parents, you don't disown your child over mistakes. Neither does your Heavenly Father! Relax, God will change your heart and sometimes you don't even know when you have changed. You're sinking foundation that falls during a whirlwind will now be a foundation that is ever lasting.

TWO HUNDRED EIGHTEEN

Luke 8:17

For nothing is hidden that will not become evident, nor anything secret that will not be known and come to light.

In Jesus name Amen

Nothing more to say on this one!!!

TWO HUNDRED NINETEEN

Psalm 30:5

For his anger lasts only a moment, but his favor lasts a lifetime; weeping may stay for the night but rejoicing comes in the morning.

In Jesus name Amen

Trust in Jesus Christ and know He keeps His word. Whatever you may be going through, Jesus is right there with you!!! Run toward God when trouble hits or when you feel you have done something wrong, He is NOT angry with you! Jump into the Lord's lap and rejoice! Whatever you're going through, "This too will pass." Run toward Jesus no matter what you have done. His arms are open for just YOU! Never run away from Him. His LOVE is unconditional. He LOVES YOU!!!!

TWO HUNDRED TWENTY

Psalms 10:4

The wicked in his proud countenance does not seek God; God is in none of his thoughts.

In Jesus name Amen

Check to see what's in your thoughts today. Only you can make that change.

TWO HUNDRED TWENTY-ONE

Isaiah 41:10

Fear not, for I am with you; be not dismayed, for I am your God; I will strengthen you, I will help you, I will uphold you with my righteous right hand.

In Jesus name Amen

Ever feel like you fail God? Ever think God will never use you? Those thoughts are lies from Satan! God is always with you! God will always strengthen you! God will always help you! God will always pick you up! Never run from God! Always run toward God! God doesn't use you because you are perfect but because you believe His word and are willing to be used by Him!

TWO HUNDRED TWENTY-TWO

Genesis 1:26

Then God said, "Let us (Jesus) make mankind in our image, in our likeness, (Jesus) so that they may rule over the fish in the sea and the birds in the sky, over the livestock and all the wild animals, and over all the creatures that move along the ground."

In Jesus name Amen

Was Jesus with God in the beginning? Here you go...YES!

TWO HUNDRED TWENTY-THREE

Matthew 24:36

But about that day or hour no one knows, not even the angels in heaven, nor the Son, but only the Father.

In Jesus name Amen

Don't even try to figure it out! People are making all kinds of guesses, and they always will. Relax and just walk with Jesus and follow His lead and His Word. No matter when Jesus comes, you'll be ready.

1. Ask Jesus into your heart.

2. Follow His lead.

3. Do His Word by Faith.

4. Always do things in Love.

Yes, love all and most of all love the unloved. Keep moving forward and always toward God! You can never go wrong!!! Stop and know Jesus loves you so much and He is coming back!!! Be ready! You don't want to miss out on this trip!

TWO HUNDRED TWENTY-FOUR

Revelation 21:4

He will wipe away every tear from their eyes, and death shall be no more, neither shall there be mourning, nor crying, nor pain anymore, for the former things have passed away.

In Jesus name Amen

A real life begins! This life is just a vapor, you see it, then it's gone! Then real life begins. Don't let anything or anybody steal your Joy. You have so much ahead of you when you are Born Again!!! Nothing to fear! Have full confidence in your Lord Jesus Christ who cannot lie!!! You already have it all! Just take time to think about. It isn't what you don't have, it's what you do have!

TWO HUNDRED TWENTY-FIVE

John 14:27

Peace I leave with you; my peace I give to you. Not as the world gives do I give to you. Let not your hearts be troubled, neither let them be afraid.

In Jesus name Amen

Take the deep peace that only God gives. Always know He is with you and loves you. God never said you will not have troubles or things that may scare you. God is saying when these things come your way, lean on Him! Let your heart be fully aware and He will help get you through these things with a deep peace in your heart.

TWO HUNDRED TWENTY-SIX

Jeremiah 29:11

For I know the plans I have for you, declares the Lord, plans for welfare and not for evil, to give you a future and a hope.

In Jesus name Amen

Waking with God is always a win-win situation. Things will happen! Things happen for those who DO walk with God and for those who DO NOT walk with God. So why walk with God? God gets you through it faster and with a better outcome and you get more sleep! Why would you walk without the most powerful hand upon your life?! Not perfect? It's ok! That's why you walk with God!

TWO HUNDRED TWENTY-SEVEN

2 Corinthians 5:7

For we live by faith, not by sight.

In Jesus name Amen

With God, it's all about trusting and believing Him FIRST. Then you'll see your prayers answered.

TWO HUNDRED TWENTY-EIGHT

Luke 18:11-13

The Pharisee stood by himself and prayed:
'God, I thank you that I am not like other
people--robbers, evildoers, adulterers--or even
like this tax collector.
I fast twice a week and give a tenth of all I
get.
"But the tax collector stood at a distance. He
would not even look up to heaven, but beat his
breast and said, 'God, have mercy on me, a
sinner.'

In Jesus name Amen

Just be humble before the Lord. He knows your
strengths and your weaknesses. Most of all, He
knows your heart. Come to the Father knowing
how much He loves you and is there for you!
God sent His son to cover your sins. So go
before God knowing He does everything in
LOVE. You're His child!

TWO HUNDRED TWENTY-NINE

Matthew 10:32-33

So everyone who acknowledges me before men, I also will acknowledge before my Father who is in heaven.
But whoever denies me before men, I also will deny before my Father who is in heaven.

In Jesus name Amen

Your LOVE for your Lord Jesus Christ should never be a private relationship and you should never feel like you can't share Him! I have heard people say, "My relationship with God is a private thing." Do you say my relationship with my children is private? Do you say my relationship with my grandchildren is private? Oh No!!! I am always sharing my love for my children and grandchildren. My love for the Lord is greater!!

YES, I will share my love for Him, and I will share His love that He has for the world. Some things should be private like your opinions and your judgements! Shut up on some things and open up on the things of God. The Bible is also beautiful!! God is Love! God's Word is alive! Your light should shine EVERYWHERE YOU GO!!

TWO HUNDRED THIRTY

Isaiah 40:8

The grass withers, the flower fades, but the word of our God will stand forever.

In Jesus name Amen

How will your world end after your grass withers and your flowers fade? Because one day they will. Will your life stand forever? It really is your choice. Know that God wants you to be forever with Him.

TWO HUNDRED THIRTY-ONE

Psalm 91:7

A thousand may fall at your side, ten thousand at your right hand, but it will not come near you.

In Jesus name Amen.

It may feel close! God says: IT WILL NOT COME NEAR YOU!! Get excited child of God... this is you HE is talking about! It is time for us to stop, read out loud, let our ears hear our very own voice saying what God says!! It doesn't take a rocket scientist to understand God's Word. It takes your Spirit, your heart and truly believing God's Word. Then the Holy Spirit will show you and teach you and guide you.

TWO HUNDRED THIRTY-TWO

Titus 3:4-7

But when the kindness and love of God our
Savior appeared,
He saved us, not because of righteous things we
had done, but because of His mercy. He saved
us through the washing of rebirth and renewal
by the Holy Spirit,
whom He poured out on us generously through
Jesus Christ our Savior,
So that, having been justified by His grace we
might become heirs having the hope of eternal
life.

In Jesus name Amen

Did you read? Jesus doesn't love us on what we
do or not do. God is love and He loves you for
you. Come as you are! Once you truly invite
Jesus into your heart you are His child. As His
child you are an heir to Him. So, step up to all
His promises, they are yours. Go and dig into
the Word and find out what is already yours!!
Yes, you are so rich!! Dig in and apply His Word
to your life.

TWO HUNDRED THIRTY-THREE

Titus 2:7

In everything set them an example by doing what is good. In your teaching show integrity, seriousness

In Jesus name Amen

Someone is always watching and listening. He knows you're not perfect. You just walk, talk and act in God's LOVE. What does love look like when you walk, talk and act it out? Love is patient, love is kind. It does not envy, it does not boast, it is not proud. It is not rude, it is not self-seeking, it is not easily angered, it keeps no record of wrongs. Love does not delight in evil but rejoices with the truth.

TWO HUNDRED THIRTY-FOUR

Proverbs 15:1

A gentle answer turns away wrath, but a harsh word stirs up anger.

In Jesus name Amen

Negativity needs to stop! Anger needs to stop! Division needs to stop You! Not your neighbor! It begins with you! Get rid of your pride and be the one with a gentle answer. We need to stop being the one that needs to be right at the cost of LOVE. Just think... in a year, will you remember the situation? Most likely NO! Let God's Word be more important than your sharp tongue to cause wrath and anger. A lesson we all can learn. Remember you are the blessed one, if YOU are the peacekeeper. Walk away from the world's way of doing things and walk away WITH more than gold and silver, God's precious blessing and His peace. Which do you choose?

TWO HUNDRED THIRTY-FIVE

Matthew 15:11

It's not what goes into your mouth that defiles you; you are defiled by the words that come out of your mouth.

In Jesus name Amen

Anything you call yourself is not what God calls you; you need to change those names. Don't defile your own self. If God says it... it is important! You are important to Him. You know the saying: "If the shoe fits?" The shoe you're trying to wear doesn't fit, kick it off and listen to God.

TWO HUNDRED THIRTY-SIX

Matthew 17:5-7

While he was still speaking, a bright cloud
covered them, and a voice from the cloud said,
"This is my Son, whom I love; with him I am
well pleased. Listen to him!"
When the disciples heard this, they fell
facedown to the ground, terrified.
But Jesus came and touched them. "Get up," he
said. "Don't be afraid."

In Jesus name Amen

What a mighty God!! God loved us so much, he
sent His son Jesus Christ to teach us how to
walk the walk, how to talk the talk and how to
love the unloved! God said, in a mighty voice to
listen to Him! His beloved son. We may not
understand all of God's ways, but we were told
to listen to Him! You know when we just step
out and listen and do His Word His way, the
outcome is so much better than we could ever
believe. Just do it by the book. One step at a
time. He is your God; He will never harm you in
any way. Step out! Step in! And LISTEN.

TWO HUNDRED THIRTY-SEVEN

Matthew 24:27

For as the lightning comes from the east and flashes to the west, so also will the coming of the Son of Man be.

In Jesus name Amen

Just be ready! No one will miss His coming! Some will be happy! Some will be sad! Which will you be?

TWO HUNDRED THIRTY-EIGHT

Proverbs 17:22

A joyful heart is good medicine, but a crushed spirit dries up the bones.

In Jesus name Amen

Have a good laugh today! Jesus is supporting you! Keep everything nice and healthy at no cost to you! Best medicine in the world!!

TWO HUNDRED THIRTY-NINE

Proverbs 18:24

A man of many companions may come to ruin, but there is a friend who sticks closer than a brother.

In Jesus name Amen

When you find that one TRUE FRIEND, God has blessed you with one of biggest blessings ever! God has done this great thing for you! You always have God that will never leave you or your TRUE FRIEND!

TWO HUNDRED FORTY

Romans 8:28

And we know that for those who love God all things work together for good, for those who are called according to his purpose.

In Jesus name Amen

When something disappoints you, just know God knows what is best for you. While your flesh man is crying out feeling disappointment, let your spirit man thank God for taking care of you. Remember He is the one that can see the future.

TWO HUNDRED FORTY-ONE

Jeremiah 29:11

For I know the plans I have for you," declares the Lord, "plans to prosper you and not to harm you, plans to give you hope and a future.

In Jesus name Amen

Just remember you may go through things and God will get you through them! He is NOT doing harm to you, nor will He send harm to you!! God gives hope and gives you a future and plans to prosper you. Have you figured out who is stealing, killing, and destroying your life? Yes, you make the final decisions but who puts thoughts in your head to do things your way and not God's way? BINGO! Satan! Read God's Word and find out God's wonderful plan for you. Go step by step and when you fall, because you will, just ask for forgiveness and begin again. God has an answer for every situation. Find the verse that will fit your situation and do it by the book! Now you're on the right path! Just do it by the BOOK!! (I picked up this saying from my Pastor. So simple to remember when life is so complicated.)

TWO HUNDRED FORTY-TWO

1 Peter 4:9

Show hospitality to one another without grumbling.

In Jesus name Amen

Make sure you're walking with the same attitude toward others like Jesus has when He is helping you.

TWO HUNDRED FORTY-THREE

Galatians 6:8

Whoever sows to please their flesh, from the flesh will reap destruction; whoever sows to please the Spirit, from the Spirit will reap eternal life.

In Jesus name Amen

Your steps to only do what YOU feel like doing will lead to destruction. The flesh cries out to satisfy what the body cries out for. When you step out and please what the spirit is leading you to do, you will receive eternal life. A life forever... and ever... and forever!

So, you will have to decide on one of these: destruction or eternal life. Remember God gives you a choice. Whether you believe it or not it's going to happen. One way or the other. Don't blame your decisions on God. God wants your love for Him to be given freely and not to be forced. People are in Hell by choice. People are in Heaven by choice. This is reality. God is guiding your heart to follow Him. He has great things awaiting you! God wants you to be with Him only if you want to be with Him. He loves you so much and wants you so much to be with Him. He hands out Grace and Mercy to YOU, brand new each day. That's the God love that is so much stronger than any flesh love.

TWO HUNDRED FORTY-FOUR

1 Corinthians 10:13

No temptation has overtaken you that is not common to man. God is faithful, and he will not let you be tempted beyond your ability, but with the temptation he will also provide the way of escape, that you may be able to endure it.

In Jesus name Amen

Satan has always used the same tricks even in the Old Testament. Find out in your situation how he used the very same thing on people in the Bible. Find out how God told them to handle it. Now when you do it God's Way, you will stop Satan in his path quickly!! Again, the authority has been given to YOU! Now take up that authority!

Forgiveness? Forgive others.

Healing? Believe you are healed.

Finances? Give.

Need blessings? Pray for others.

Do it by the book and Satan must flee!!!!

TWO HUNDRED FORTY-FIVE

1Timothy 2:1-2

First of all, then, I urge that supplications,
prayers, intercessions, and thanksgivings be
made for all people,
for kings and all who are in high positions, that
we may lead a peaceful and quiet life, godly and
dignified in every way.

In Jesus name Amen

Pray, then go vote!!

TWO HUNDRED FORTY-SIX

Psalm 46:10

Be still, and know that I am God. I will be exalted among the nations, I will be exalted in the earth!

In Jesus name Amen

God's Word does not come back void. God will be exalted in the Earth!!! Get excited!!!

TWO HUNDRED FORTY-SEVEN

Acts 4:30

While you stretch out your hand to heal, and signs and wonders are performed through the name of your holy servant Jesus.

In Jesus name Amen

How powerful is the name of Jesus? Signs and wonders are performed in His name and His name alone! Jesus handed over the POWER to you, the believer!!!

TWO HUNDRED FORTY-EIGHT

James 4:10

Humble yourselves before the Lord, and he will lift you up.

In Jesus name Amen

Work unto the Lord and He will lift you up. Lift others up and God will lift you up. Just humble yourself and God will do His part. Trust Him!

TWO HUNDRED FORTY-NINE

John 14:27

Peace I leave with you; my peace I give to you. Not as the world gives do I give to you. Let not your hearts be troubled, neither let them be afraid.

In Jesus name Amen

Okay, time for YOU to rest when it comes to this crazy world. Take this PEACE Jesus left for YOU, take this PEACE Jesus gives to YOU and truly rest. Jesus tells us His PEACE is not from this world, it is truly different. How do you find this PEACE? You need to find your quiet time each day just for YOU and God to spend time together. Read His Word and discover a new PEACE that comes from the heart of Jesus straight into YOUR heart. YOU can have PEACE when this world has none! From the mouth of your Lord Jesus Christ, He tells YOU not to let YOUR heart be troubled or afraid. Why does God tell us this? He knows something we don't! Walk by Faith and trust in Him!

TWO HUNDRED FIFTY

2 Timothy 1:7

For God gave us a spirit not of fear but of power and love and self-control.

In Jesus name Amen

Who wants to waste their time on FEAR?

Who wants to feed their FEAR?

FEAR is: False Evidence Appearing Real!

This spirit is not from God, no good thing will come out of this spirit, only steps to stop you from living and moving forward. Walk in the POWER that God gives you and grow in LOVE and SELF CONTROL. You will walk into blessing that keeps on giving and a life that Keeps on growing toward God!

TWO HUNDRED FIFTY-ONE

James 1:22

Do not merely listen to the word, and so deceive yourselves. Do what it says.

In Jesus name Amen

Are we able to do what the word says? God says yes! What will you tell God when you are face to face with Him?

TWO HUNDRED FIFTY-TWO

Luke 21:28

Now when these things begin to take place, straighten up and raise your heads, because your redemption is drawing near."

In Jesus Name Amen

Get ready my friends. These things must happen! Get excited! Get past your own ideas of how things should happen and focus on the coming of our Lord Jesus Christ because He is coming back! Are you truly ready? Games will soon be over.

TWO HUNDRED FIFTY-THREE

1 John 3:7

Dear children, do not let anyone lead you astray. The one who does what is right is righteous, just as he is righteous.

In Jesus name Amen

Do what is right in God's eyes. The god of this world, Satan wants to lead you away from God, away from His blessings, away from God's protection. Away from His future for you. The Man who does right is in right standing with God. Always check God's Word against your thoughts so you will not be led astray. God will show you the right path, but God does not make you walk this path. Perfect is not the path. Your Faithfulness in Jesus Christ is the right path! Stay strong!!!! It is all worth it!!!!

TWO HUNDRED FIFTY-FOUR

Isaiah 14:15-16

But you are brought down to the realm of the dead, to the depths of the pit.
Those who see you stare at you, they ponder your fate: "Is this the man who shook the earth and made kingdoms tremble

In Jesus name Amen

Who made Satan more powerful after Jesus Christ gave us all authority over him? You did! Who is making Satan big, bad, red with horns and muscles? You are! When you see Satan, you will see a weak, powerless, scared Angel that was stripped of everything.

Get back into your position with God! If Satan was more powerful than God, he would have kicked God out of Heaven. You have AUTHORITY OVER SATAN!! Walk it out by Faith in Jesus Christ! Talk it out by Faith in Jesus Christ! Finally start believing what the Bible says and put 100 percent of your faith back into Lord Jesus Christ and live it!

TWO HUNDRED FIFTY-FIVE

Psalm 86:7

In the day of my trouble I shall call upon You,
For You will answer me.

In Jesus name Amen

I know things in this world can be really hard at
times. Remember You can call on the Lord and
HE WILL answer. Just remember to take time
out to listen. Step into your closet, close the
door and keep the world out of your spiritual
world until you hear from God. He is already
there waiting for you with your answer. He
loves you so much! Why would He give His son
for you then not give you an answer?

TWO HUNDRED FIFTY-SIX

Corinthians 13:4-7

Love is patient, love is kind. It does not envy, it does not boast, it is not proud.
It does not dishonor others, it is not self-seeking, it is not easily angered, it keeps no record of wrongs.
Love does not delight in evil but rejoices with the truth.
It always protects, always trusts, always hopes, always perseveres.

In Jesus name Amen

My dear brothers and sisters, take note of this: Everyone should be quick to listen, slow to speak and slow to become angry, because human anger does not produce the righteousness that God desires.

1. Be QUICK to listen.
2. Be SLOW to speak.
3. Be SLOW to become angry.

Maybe I should send this one out once a week? Lol Remember when we find out God's Way, it's the only way to do things! Praying for you, my sweet friend!!

TWO HUNDRED FIFTY-SEVEN

Romans 8:38-39

For I am sure that neither death nor life, nor angels nor rulers, nor things present nor things to come, nor powers,
nor height nor depth, nor anything else in all creation, will be able to separate us from the love of God in Christ Jesus our Lord.

In Jesus name Amen

Rejoice!! And just rest! Everything is going to be alright, as long as you are born again! Ask Jesus to come in your heart and be Lord over your life. Ask for forgiveness of your sins in Jesus' name. Blessed...a sure thing! Heaven, love, peace, having a reunion with loved ones!! All good and great things in Heaven! I really want to see you there!

TWO HUNDRED FIFTY-EIGHT

1 John 1:9

If we confess our sins, he is faithful and just to forgive us our sins and to cleanse us from all unrighteousness.

In Jesus name Amen

Did you read that? God cleanses us from ALL unrighteousness if we just ask Him. Satan will come back and tell you that you are not forgiven! He wants you to keep a wall up between you and God! If you are like me, you can't count or remember every one of your sins. So just ask God to forgive you of all sins in Jesus name, and His love for you is so true and deep as fast as you ask for forgiveness, He has washed you white as snow! God doesn't remember your sins, so why should you?! When Satan comes around to remind you of what you have done in the past, and trust me he will try, you just remind him of his future. The Lake of fire! YOU ARE FORGIVEN once and for ALL!

TWO HUNDRED FIFTY-NINE

Matthew 28:20

Teaching them to observe all that I have commanded you. And behold, I am with you always, to the end of the age."

In Jesus name Amen

Do you even have to ask God to be with you? Do you have to beg God to be with you? Do you have to invite God to be with you? When you are born again, NO!! God tells us: "I am with you always!" ALWAYS: at all times and on all occasions!! Now believe what God says. He is right there, just talk to Him like your closest friend. The difference is God is always there when your friend can not always be there.

TWO HUNDRED SIXTY

Jude 20-21

But ye, beloved, building up yourselves on your most holy faith, praying in the Holy Ghost, keep yourselves in the love of God, looking for the mercy of our Lord Jesus Christ unto eternal life.

In Jesus name Amen

The love God has for you has already been poured into your heart. He has never taken it away. If you are not feeling the Love of God, the verse says for YOU to build yourself up and pray in the most Holy Ghost (in tongues). It's for everyone, just ask and receive it. God does not have favorites. It is for you. After praying, keep yourself in the love of God. Read His Word that's in the Bible and know that He has made it possible just for you. Say what God says about loving you. You are so deeply loved by God. Not feeling the love from God? Open your mouth and read His Word out loud. It's not what you do or don't do. He knows you and loves you. Satan is telling you that God doesn't love you because of your bad behavior. When did Satan ever tell the truth? God is still in Love with you, fall back in Love with Him or work on building it stronger.

TWO HUNDRED SIXTY-ONE

Ephesians 6:13

Therefore take up the whole armor of God, that you may be able to withstand in the evil day, and having done all, to stand firm.

In Jesus name Amen

Jesus is not shocked about these evil days so neither should you be. He made a way for you during the evil days if you follow His instructions. Put on the armor then stand and don't move away from God's Word. Time to put on the Word. Wear it, be it, speak it and do it everywhere you go!! You will stand strong and confident as a Christian. God has given you everything you need for each day. Smile and trust God as you walk by His instruction's day by day.

TWO HUNDRED SIXTY-TWO

Colossians 3:15

Let the peace of Christ rule in your hearts, since as members of one body you were called to peace. And be thankful.

In Jesus name Amen

Who rules your heart? FEAR? Or PEACE? Peace is from God. We are so trained in life if we aren't fearful or worried about something, we don't care. Those are lies from Hell. When you have the Peace of God in your heart you can go through anything and know everything is going to be alright. Your Faith in God gives you the rest and peace. Not there yet? You will be! Oh, what a feeling! Let God's Words come out of your mouth and peace and thanksgiving is what you will feel in your heart.

TWO HUNDRED SIXTY-THREE

Proverbs 3:3

Let love and faithfulness never leave you; bind them around your neck, write them on the tablet of your heart.

In Jesus name Amen

A lot of things you may lose but the most important thing not to lose is LOVE and FAITHFULNESS!

TWO HUNDRED SIXTY-FOUR

Psalm 31:14

But I trust in you, O Lord; I say, "You are my God."

In Jesus name Amen

When was the last time you sat down and closed the world out and really said to the Lord Jesus Christ, "You are my GOD!" This is a special time to give Him your love and the words that are in your heart that are only for your God.

TWO HUNDRED SIXTY-FIVE

Proverbs 4:23

Above all else, guard your heart, for everything you do flows from it.

In Jesus name Amen

Guarding your heart doesn't mean guarding it against people and cutting them off. That is not God's Way to treat people. That's another subject. To guard your heart means to guard against it getting: "hardened, stony, and against worries." All these things steal God's Word from your heart and the Word cannot grow or even the understanding of the Word. Stay HUMBLE, put others ahead of yourself so your heart stays soft. Stay in FAITH so the worries of this world cannot steal the peace of God in your heart. Don't be that "I KNOW IT ALL" person. This will only stop the understanding of God's Word. Satan is working overtime to steal the good ground God gives you. When you became born again, that's when God made the new heart in you. So don't ask God to create a new heart in you because He already has. It's your job to keep your heart soft and rich which brings a great flow of good fruit. Love, peace, caring, and giving, that's God's Way of doing things. God's Word is now growing! It's worth protecting and guarding. When you are moving toward guarding your heart in the right way, so much good fruit comes from God... to you! It's not what you do, but what flows from your heart out of your mouth that is so much more important.

TWO HUNDRED SIXTY-SIX

Psalm 4:8

In peace I will lie down and sleep, for you alone, LORD, make me dwell in safety.

In Jesus name Amen

Need a good night's sleep? Fill your mind with sweet and gentle words from God. So easy to do today, with ear pods and YouTube, you can find readings of the Word. Rest and sleep with good going in and have a great night's sleep. You'll find peace your sleep will be sweet.

TWO HUNDRED SIXTY-SEVEN

Proverbs 4:7

Wisdom is the principal thing; therefore get wisdom: and with all thy getting get understanding.

In Jesus name Amen

Spending time in the Bible sure gives you a lot of Wisdom. How are you doing?

TWO HUNDRED SIXTY-EIGHT

Psalm 30:5

For His anger is but for a moment, His favor is for life; weeping may endure for a night, but joy comes in the morning.

In Jesus name Amen

This is your Lord Jesus Christ speaking to YOU! His favor is for a lifetime! Joy comes in the morning! His anger is only for a moment! Weeping only endures for a night! Go ahead and rest in His arms and know He does answer with the best answer that you need! Rest and trust.

TWO HUNDRED SIXTY-NINE

Psalms 91:5-7

You will not fear the terror of night, nor the arrow that flies by day,
nor the pestilence that stalks in the darkness, nor the plague that destroys at midday. 7 A thousand may fall at your side, ten thousand at your right hand, but it will not come near you.

In Jesus name Amen

Proverbs 18:21

The tongue has the power of life and death, and those who love it will eat its fruit.

In Jesus name Amen

Trouble will come! Do not be full of fear! Everyday check your armor of God and make sure it's in place. Take heed the words you speak from YOUR mouth the words will be LIFE or DEATH. Armor: 1. Salvation. (being born again) 2. Righteous. (Know that you're right standing with God because Jesus gave you this!) 3. Be truthful. 4. Walk in peace. (Feet, shoes.) 5. Your FAITH. (The shield) 6. Be a doer of the Word. (Sword.) 7. Stay alert. (Pray in all occasions, for all the LORD's people.)

TWO HUNDRED SEVENTY

Matthew 12:33

Either make the tree good and its fruit good, or make the tree bad and its fruit bad, for the tree is known by its fruit.

In Jesus name Amen

Can I judge that you are going to Heaven or Hell? Not my job! Can I judge you by your fruit? Yes, I can listen to the words that come out of your mouth and judge if I want to hang out with you or not. Am I allowed to mistreat you? NO! Walk in love always.

TWO HUNDRED SEVENTY-ONE

2 Corinthians 5:7

For we walk by faith, not by sight

In Jesus name Amen

Walking by sight is not how we are to know Jesus. It's ok to have goose bumps sometimes, it's ok to feel the awareness of God. He does manifest Himself to us that way and it's great!! To know God by Faith without any feelings of awareness or without the goosebumps is the strongest way to walk. Walk by Faith is to know Him spiritually. You need to get out of the flesh and know that by Faith, your God is always with you! His Word is always true! He is always listening to you! Now when you know God is truly with you without needing all the emotions, you are walking by faith and not by feelings, the way God truly wants you to know Him. Read God's Word and apply it. Walk by faith because it's not up to you to make the Word work, God has already put this into action when you activate His Word by your FAITH!!!

TWO HUNDRED SEVENTY-TWO

John 14:12

Truly, truly, I say to you, whoever believes in me will also do the works that I do; and greater works than these will he do, because I am going to the Father.

In Jesus name Amen

Are you a whoever? Do you believe in Jesus Christ? Then Jesus is talking to YOU! He will use the most unlikely people to do His works on this Earth. Yes, ME! Yes, YOU!

TWO HUNDRED SEVENTY-THREE

Matthew 25:35

For I was hungry and you gave me food, I was thirsty and you gave me drink, I was a stranger and you welcomed me.

In Jesus name Amen

"It's not about you!" Look around and see who needs a touch from God. Then you go fix the need. You will be blessed! Can't outgive God no matter what you give from your pocket, your household, or your heart!!!

TWO HUNDRED SEVENTY-FOUR

Psalm 29:11

The Lord gives strength to his people; the Lord blesses his people with peace.

In Jesus name Amen

Why does God give HIS people strength and Peace at the same time? For days like these, that are so uncertain. True Christians will be made to be strong and have peace through anything. They will be singing praise during these hard times!! People who pretend to be Christian will be left with traditions or simple religion. The world does not understand how important it is to study, read and apply the Word of God in their lives. They are ignorant (lacking knowledge) and cannot understand the Word of the Lord. God will give HIS people wisdom and strength like no other to be able to go through what is coming. If you are scared, unsure, no peace and just decide to go with the flow of the world, you are the one that will be in trouble! Time is over for sugar coating things so no one will be offended. Now is the time to dig deep in God's Word and plant His Word in your heart. Then when hard times come, what is in your heart will flow out your mouth and that's where your strength comes from and your peace!

TWO HUNDRED SEVENTY-FIVE

Proverbs 14:7-9

Walk away from the company of fools, for you cannot find insight in their words.
It takes wisdom for the clever to understand the path they are on, but the fool is deceived by his own foolishness.
Fools make a mockery of guilt and repentance but those who do what is right receive special standing.

In Jesus name Amen

Do you make fun of repentance, or do you know someone who does? WALK AWAY FROM these FOOLS! If you're the fool, turn away from these ways and follow the Word of God! God is Faithful!! For those that have wisdom in their hearts, they will ask for forgiveness and will know right then and there that they have been forgiven. Oh, how blessed we are to RECEIVE special standing with Jesus Christ. Who cares what the world thinks of us? Let us be more concerned with Jesus Christ!! True Wisdom!! When things get tough, the true children of God will not be moved from God's Word, even if people make fun of us.

TWO HUNDRED SEVENTY-SIX

Matthew 5:11

Blessed are ye, when men shall revile you, and persecute you, and shall say all manner of evil against you falsely, for my sake.

In Jesus name Amen

God's way of doing things is backward to our thinking. Jesus' Mother, Mary, told the servant to do whatever Jesus says. Jesus told them to fill each water pot with water because all the wine was gone. This really did not make any sense! They did what Jesus said and when they poured the water out of the water pots into the guest cups it was the best wine ever!! God said, when all matter of evil comes against you don't feel sorry for yourself! Know you are so blessed!! Walk in Faith and not by sight! Things are going to be alright!

TWO HUNDRED SEVENTY-SEVEN

Proverbs 22:6

Train up a child in the way he should go; even when he is old he will not depart from it.

In Jesus name Amen

Are you doing your part to share Jesus and God's Word with your children? (No matter how old they are.) How about your Grandbabies? Teach them, train them in the way they SHOULD go, and they will RETURN! Invest in the most precious, most important road you can and that is the road to Jesus Christ. Their future is in your hands.

TWO HUNDRED SEVENTY-EIGHT

Ephesians 2:8

For by grace are ye saved through faith; and that not of yourselves: it is the gift of God:

In Jesus name Amen

The most precious gift of all, in our celebration in this season was sent to us from Heaven above. (Truth) His name is Jesus! He came and gave us all He had. Has anyone ever given all they had to give you a gift? I doubt it. You want a gift that keeps on giving, giving in grace, giving in love, giving in forgiveness, giving in healing? The gift goes on and on. The gift is so special you get it every day of the year! When you hear that whisper saying: "ask me to come in your heart" and when you do, you will become a child of God, and this wonderful gift is all yours for being His child. Yes, let's celebrate this gift! The greatest gift ever is JESUS CHRIST! This gift has no conditions. This gift is freely yours as a child of the Highest God, He has given His Son for you, just as you are! COME! COME as you are!

TWO HUNDRED SEVENTY-NINE

Psalm 150:4

Praise him with tambourine and dance; praise him with strings and pipe!

In Jesus name Amen

God said, "don't forget to assemble together."
Going to church should be a time to party!
Come party! Praise! Dance! And sing! Worship!
Then go home and continue!

TWO HUNDRED EIGHTY

Romans 8:31

What then shall we say to these things? If God is for us, who can be against us?

In Jesus name Amen

Which part do YOU not understand?

TWO HUNDRED EIGHTY-ONE

Ephesians 2:10

For we are God's handiwork, created in Christ Jesus to do good works, which God prepared in advance for us to do.

In Jesus name Amen

You are not a mistake! God had plans for you before you were born. You were thought of, and plans were made just for you. You were created on purpose for a purpose! Are you special to God? Oh yes you are!! YES! YOU!

TWO HUNDRED EIGHTY-TWO

Romans 10:17

So faith comes from hearing, and hearing through the word of Christ.

In Jesus name Amen

Your faith needs more than just reading off the internet. Faith comes from hearing, and hearing THROUGH the word of CHRIST! Time to do things God's way. Assemble yourself with other believers and unbelievers who want to know more of who Jesus Christ is. Just do it by the book! (My Pastor says this and does the dance.) Come and see! Find a place to receive His Great Word each Sunday!!!

TWO HUNDRED EIGHTY-THREE

1 Corinthians 3:16

Know ye not that ye are the temple of God, and that the Spirit of God dwelleth in you?

In Jesus name Amen

Once you are born again, the Spirit of God really comes alive inside you. He hears what you hear. He sees what you see. You are a TEMPLE! That's where the Holy Spirit lives! Be so humble and honored that God loves you so much. Of all places, the Holy Spirit lives inside of YOU!!

TWO HUNDRED EIGHTY-FOUR

Acts 1:8

But you will receive power when the Holy Spirit comes on you; and you will be my witnesses in Jerusalem, and in all Judea and Samaria, and to the ends of the earth.

In Jesus name Amen

You have POWER when Holy Spirit comes in you. This POWER is to do the Lord's Work. Do you have POWER? God is the one who said it! A BIG YES! God does not lie. Meditate on this verse for a while. Satan does not want you to get this understanding in your heart. Once you do, Satan no longer has POWER over you!

TWO HUNDRED EIGHTY-FIVE

Psalm 136:26

Give thanks to the God of heaven, for his steadfast love endures forever.

In Jesus name Amen

And you think your behavior has stopped God's love for you? His unmovable LOVE endures forever for YOU! His arms are always open towards YOU. Never let shame or doubt stop you from talking with God. Those are tools the enemy uses to stop you from going to God. Remember the enemy hates you!

TWO HUNDRED EIGHTY-SIX

Romans 10:9-10

If you declare with your mouth, "Jesus is Lord," and believe in your heart that God raised him from the dead, you will be saved.
For it is with your heart that you believe and are justified, and it is with your mouth that you profess your faith and are saved.

In Jesus name Amen

By something you cannot see but you believe in. You were saved, it was faith! The same Faith is inside you to lay hands on the sick and see them recover. Don't wait for someone with stronger faith than you. YOU are that person! You believed you were saved without seeing faith, without seeing God. When you believe, your faith kicks in. (The faith God gave you at birth.) You were saved!! Hallelujah! Believe and let your faith in God kick in! It's God who honors His word by your Faith. The only thing you need to have, is… faith and believe the same way you were saved. Time for Born Again children of God to stand up and show Satan who is more powerful!! YOU! If we all did what God said: "lay hands on the sick and they WILL RECOVER" people will get their eye's back on God. We need to open the box and step out of the box for God!! Spend more time with God and His word and watch God use YOU! Hey, He is using me, who would of guessed? A New You for God!

TWO HUNDRED EIGHTY-SEVEN

Psalm 9:10

And those who know your name put their trust in you, for you, O LORD, have not forsaken those who seek you."

In Jesus name Amen

"For THOSE." That's YOU! Who put THEIR trust in you, O LORD. The LORD will never FORSAKE US! Every hour read this and chew on this meat of the Lord's. Your fear of anything will not take a room in your heart anymore! Hallelujah to our Lord Jesus Christ! His Word will endure forever! So will you when you seek Him every day!

TWO HUNDRED EIGHTY-EIGHT

Hebrews 12:2

Looking unto Jesus, the author and finisher of our faith, who for the joy that was set before Him endured the cross, despising the shame, and has sat down at the right hand of the throne of God.

In Jesus name Amen

Who is the Author of your Faith? Jesus. He created this faith and placed it inside of you. Hey, His power goes with this faith He created. So, step out and with His Faith He placed inside you and do what He says to do! It's His power doing the healing. What you are doing is taking the Authority.

TWO HUNDRED EIGHTY-NINE

Psalm 21:13

Be thou exalted, LORD, in thine own strength:
so will we sing and praise thy power.

In Jesus name Amen

Rejoice! Rejoice! In private and in public unto
the Lord!! God's Power is more than our brain
can understand. We may not understand, but
that doesn't change the fact that there is
wonderful POWER above all! Everything must
bow down to the Power of our Lord. We will
praise your Love, your Mercy, your Grace and
your Power throughout our land, Almighty God.
There is nothing like you Jesus Christ! Nothing!

TWO HUNDRED NINETY

Proverbs 6:6-8

Go to the ant, you sluggard; consider its ways
and be wise!
It has no commander, no overseer or ruler,
yet it stores its provisions in summer and
gathers its food at harvest.

In Jesus name Amen

Which one are you? The ant? The sluggard?
Each has its reward.

TWO HUNDRED NINETY-ONE

1 Chronicles 16:31

Let the heavens rejoice, let the earth be glad; let them say among the nations, "The LORD reigns!"

In Jesus name Amen

Need something to get you through some darkness? Sing a song unto the Lord. Sing and praise Him. Put this verse to music and to your voice. Sing, sing, sing and watch your darkness slip away! Sing, sing, sing every day, the darker your day seems the longer you keep singing!!! Next you will have a skip in your walk! A hip hop to your walk. Sounds a little crazy. Don't do things the world's way. Do it by the book - God's way!

TWO HUNDRED NINETY-TWO

James 1:6

But when you ask, you must believe and not doubt, because the one who doubts is like a wave of the sea, blown and tossed by the wind.

In Jesus name Amen

Doubt is placed in your mind by Satan. Satan is watching and listening to use your flesh and waiting to use it against you. Just because you have doubt toward God doesn't mean you need to follow that doubt and give Satan permission to toss your life into the wind. Crush those doubts that Satan is trying to use to take you down! Open the Bible and read out loud what God says about your situation. Let your very own ears hear what God has said. Run Satan right out of your mind!!! Don't let doubt have any room in your head! It only steals from you and keeps on stealing. No vacancy! Throw doubt out to the curb!!!

TWO HUNDRED NINETY-THREE

Hebrews 2:1

Therefore we must pay much closer attention to what we have heard, lest we drift away from it.

In Jesus name Amen

Time to get serious and really meditate on each Word of God. The world has drifted away from God. Let's make sure we stay the course. When you read the Word, apply it and live it! Not only on Sundays or when you know someone is watching. The time is NOW, my friends. Applying it WILL keep you in the protection of God.

TWO HUNDRED NINETY-FOUR

Philippians 4:6-7

Do not be anxious about anything, but in everything by prayer and supplication with thanksgiving. let your request be made known to God.
And the peace of God, which surpasses all understanding, will guard your hearts and your minds in Christ Jesus.

In Jesus name Amen

Which one have you forgotten? Examine yourself honestly and humble yourself before God. If you are lined up with the Word of God, you will be given peace that is far from your understanding. The world has no peace, but with God you have peace that guides your heart and your mind. We, His children have much FAVOR!

TWO HUNDRED NINETY-FIVE

Acts 1:8

But you will receive power when the Holy Spirit
has come upon you, and you will be my
witnesses in Jerusalem and in all Judea and
Samaria, and to the end of the earth."

In Jesus name Amen

The Holy Spirit lives inside of you if you're born
again. This is the same power that Jesus had.
Jesus is now in Heaven. Jesus said, you WILL
receive power when you receive the Holy Spirit!
Jesus does not lie. What are you doing with that
power and authority that He has given to you?

TWO HUNDRED NINETY-SIX

Ezekiel 2:1

And he said to me, "Son of man, stand on your feet, and I will speak with you." And he said to me, "Son of man, stand on your feet, and I will speak with you."

In Jesus name Amen.

Stand up, children of God!!!

TWO HUNDRED NINETY-SEVEN

Galatians 5:1

For freedom Christ has set us free; stand firm therefore, and do not submit again to a yoke of slavery.

In Jesus name Amen

Jesus and His Word equal freedom! Don't let Satan bark orders that you are sick, or that you are nothing! Or the lies that you cannot be loved! Especially when he tries to convince you that God's Word is dead!! That is slavery!!!!

What are you to do? STAND! STAND FIRM!!!! STAND, CHILD OF GOD!!!! Fear is not of GOD! STAND FIRM on GOD'S WORD!! NOW and GOING FORWARD! If God is against it, then we are against it. BE FIRM in YOUR STAND with GOD!

TWO HUNDRED NINETY-EIGHT

2 Timothy 1:7

For God gave us a spirit not of fear but of power and love and a sound mind.

In Jesus name Amen

If you are in fear, it has been given to you by Satan and you took it. God has given us power over Satan! The question is, which power are you going to take and live by? Replace what Satan is saying with the Words God is saying or with the Words He has already said. Not sure what Words to use? Open your Bible and start a new and wonderful way to live in this crazy world, with the power from God to us. The power of Love and self-control will stop fear.

TWO HUNDRED NINETY-NINE

Mark 6:31

And he said to them, "Come away by yourselves to a desolate place and rest a while." For many were coming and going, and they had no leisure even to eat.

In Jesus name Amen

Okay, make time for you to really rest! Things can get so crazy, and we need to get away from everyone to really rest. It's okay. Tell everyone God's Words are wisdom. We are going to apply His Word to our lives. Tell your friends to do the same.

THREE HUNDRED

Luke 4:6

And the devil said to Him (Jesus) I will give to You all this authority, and its glory; for it has been delivered to me, and I give it to whom I wish.

In Jesus name Amen

This power was given to Adam, and he gave it to Satan. Now, Satan is trying to get Jesus to bow to him and make Jesus fall like Adam did and keep this authority over us forever! It didn't work!!! Jesus decided to stay faithful to His Father in Heaven. Jesus took the beating and gave His blood for us, and he didn't stop there! Jesus died, went to Hell, and told Satan I came to strip you of all Authority and take away your glory. Jesus had no sin, so He had the right to take it back. Jesus came back to earth and when He was going back to God His Father He said, I gave YOU all authority to trample on Satan. Why are you fearful? You are more powerful than Satan! Now take control over Satan and show your authority. Show it in your eyes, in your voice and in your faithfulness unto the Lord! Wake up, church, and stand for the Lord! Satan hates me for this!!! He knows my name! Know who you are in Jesus!

THREE HUNDRED ONE

Psalm 37:5

Commit your way to the Lord; trust in him, and he will act.

In Jesus name Amen

Here is your part:

Number One - To commit your way to His Way.
Number Two -TRUST In Him...ALWAYS.

Now here is God's part:
HE WILL ACT! Hallelujah! And HE WILL!! People of God: worry and concern IS NOT your part! I heard my Pastor say today: "Trust God," "Trust God." I read in the Bible that GOD WILL ACT. GOD WILL ACT. Stop that unbelief. Stop the pity party. Find a church that is open and let's stand together in every state of America. Let's assemble and show the world you believe your Almighty God! And by your Faith and your action, they too will be drawn to God and have peace and hope. Most people who have stopped going to church will not return because their flesh is more important than to honor God. Satan has won if you continue this. These are the days you need to go to church and not stay

home. If you never went to church, now is the time to GO! Hear the Word of the Lord!

THREE HUNDRED TWO

2 Corinthians 10:4

For the weapons of our warfare are not of the flesh but have divine power to destroy strongholds.

Luke 9:1

And He called the twelve together and gave them power and authority over all demons and to cure diseases.

In Jesus name Amen

Warfare isn't with people. (Satan will cause divisions between people and laugh) let's not destroy people. So, our weapons are used for the dark strongholds. (Satan's ugly stuff.) We have been given divine power to destroy it. Yep, that's you!!! This is what Jesus has given to you!!! Power, authority and to cure disease all in the name of Jesus! Yep, that's YOU! Believe, trust, and have boldness all in Jesus' name.

THREE HUNDRED THREE

Daniel 3:24-26

Shadrach, Meshach, and Abednego, Then Nebuchadnezzar the king was astonished, and rose up in haste, and spoke, and said unto his counsellors, Did not we cast three men bound into the midst of the fire? They answered and said unto the king, True, O king.
He answered and said, Look, I see four men loose, walking in the midst of the fire, and they have no hurt; and the form of the fourth is like the Son of God.
Then Nebuchadnezzar came near to the mouth of the burning fiery furnace, and spoke, and said, Shadrach, Meshach, and Abednego, ye servants of the most high God, come forth, and come hither. Then Shadrach, Meshach, and Abednego, came forth of the midst of the fire.

In Jesus name Amen

When the fire of this world is trying to consume you, stand your ground and stand for God! Jesus is with you like He was with the three men who would not bow to any God but the true God! Knowing who their God was they CARE LESS and TRUST God. They didn't even give attention to the heat/fire!! With God all things are possible, it's above your thinking!!

The three men did not run out of that fire. They just came forth. They showed no fear at the beginning or at the end. Get to know who and what your God can do and will do for you. God is the same yesterday, today and tomorrow. CARE LESS and TRUST GOD! (Thank you, Pastor.)

THREE HUNDRED FOUR

Hebrews 9:28

So Christ, having been offered once to bear the sins of many, will appear a second time, not to deal with sin but to save those who are eagerly waiting for him.

In Jesus name Amen

Party time! Party time! Will you be ready? Are you eagerly waiting? You have to RSVP to go. Accept the invitation and follow up by accepting the Lord Jesus in your life and ask forgiveness. You now are a VIP!! Oh, you get a mansion for keeps.

THREE HUNDRED FIVE

Philippians 2:13

Because God is always at work in you to make you willing and able to obey his own purpose.

In Jesus name Amen

You are a new man/woman when you are born again. God puts His desires in your heart and before you know it you are replacing your ugly stuff with His pleasure. You don't have to work at changing. Read His Word and get to know Him and it just happens. Doing things God's way sure does make your heart really live. Enjoy your walk with God, it only gets better and better if you don't faint and give up.

THREE HUNDRED SIX

John 15:15

I no longer call you servants, because a servant does not know his master's business. Instead, I have called you friends, for everything that I learned from my Father I have made known to you.

In Jesus name Amen

Want to know what the Father Has told Jesus, His son? Read the Bible daily and you will know the Will of the Father. Study and meditate and you too will know that Jesus hasn't hidden anything from you. The saying that says: "God works in mysterious ways" is not from God! A lie to keep you from searching for the true answers from God. By opening your Bible, you can learn how Jesus tells you to be healed, be blessed, walk in peace and EVERYTHING that pertains to life. The more YOU dig into God's Word, the more you learn. Just keep digging...all your answers are right there in the Bible.

THREE HUNDRED SEVEN

Psalm 91:15

When he calls to me, I will answer him; I will be
with him in trouble; I will rescue him and honor
him.

In Jesus name Amen

Did you ever think that while you honor God,
He is honoring YOU? When you are in trouble,
He will rescue YOU. When YOU call on Him, He
answers YOU. Oh, how He loves YOU!

THREE HUNDRED EIGHT

1 Samuel 16:7

But the Lord said to Samuel, "Do not look on his appearance or on the height of his stature, because I have rejected him. For the Lord sees not as man sees: man looks on the outward appearance, but the Lord looks on the heart."

In Jesus name Amen

A good lesson for all of us! Yes, YOU who have little, but a big heart and a true heart for the Lord will be picked by the Lord to do His work. Don't be surprised... instead, be ready!

THREE HUNDRED NINE

1 Peter 4:15

But let none of you suffer as a murderer, or as a thief, or as an evildoer, or as a busybody in other men's matters.

In Jesus name Amen

In being a murderer, a thief, an evildoer, or a busybody, you cannot keep doing these things and Glorify God! The price you pay for these things is rightfully due. It is very interesting that the busybody is included with this group. Take care of that beam of wood in your eye before checking your neighbor's eye for a splinter. Learn and grow with the Word of the Lord and YOU will change your life. You will find a deep joy like you have never felt before.

THREE HUNDRED TEN

John 10:10

The thief comes only to steal and kill and destroy; I have come that they may have life, and have it to the full.

In Jesus name Amen

Let's get this straight: Who comes to steal your money, kill your health, and destroy your peace and love? Oh, it's Satan! He has been uncovered! So, let's get real here! Jesus never came to steal your money. Jesus never came to kill your health. Jesus never came to destroy your peace or love!!! Jesus came that you may have life and have it to the fullest!!! Stand your ground and quit accepting everything Satan wants to put on you. Find out what God is doing and saying and that's what you do and speak - Make it line up with GOD. Isn't that what children do? Wake up, America! Wake up, people! Wake up, Children of God! Wake up in your own household! NOW is the time that YOU act! YOU say and YOU be what our Father God says YOU are!!!!

THREE HUNDRED ELEVEN

Philippians 2:14-16

Do all things without complaining and
disputing,
that you may become blameless and harmless,
children of God without fault in the midst of a
crooked and perverse generation, among whom
you shine as lights in the world,
holding fast the word of life, so that I may
rejoice in the day of Christ that I have not run
in vain or labored in vain.

In Jesus name Amen

Don't be so hard on yourself when you hear
yourself start to complain (or have those bad
thoughts). Just stop when you realize you're
doing it. Close your mouth and take a deep
breath. Start over with words that would please
God. We are here to please our Lord, not our
flesh. These words are for you to take seriously
and apply them to your life every day. It will
change your whole day, your heart, and your
whole life!

THREE HUNDRED TWELVE

Jeremiah 2:32

Does a young woman forget her jewelry? Does a bride hide her wedding dress? Yet for years on end my people have forgotten me.

1 Timothy 2:1-2

I urge, then, first of all, that petitions, prayers, intercession and thanksgiving be made for all people
for kings and all those in authority, that we may live peaceful and quiet lives in all Godliness and Holiness

In Jesus name Amen

Let's put God first again. Please Pray for our leadership. Let us return to God and return to praying for our leaders. Our leaders are making a lot of decisions in the United States that are far from God. They have forgotten the Lord. Let us come together interceding prayer for all our leaders. God can send each of our leaders a laborer that they will listen to. If we don't help with the problems, then we are part of the problem. It's not important at this stage that we like them or dislike them. The most important above all is that we do as God has instructed us to do.

THREE HUNDRED THIRTEEN

Malachi 3:11

And I will rebuke the devourer for your sakes, and he shall not destroy the fruits of your ground; neither shall your vine cast her fruit before the time in the field, saith the LORD of hosts.

In Jesus name Amen

If you tithe and give offerings on every paycheck, you don't have to rebuke Satan to take his hands off your increase. When you give your tithe and offering, your finances are now in the hands of God. Who better to guard your money, your time and service then God?! Rest, trust God and GIVE unto HIM.

THREE HUNDRED FOURTEEN

Matthew 12:14

Then the Pharisees went out, and held a council against him, how they might destroy him.

In Jesus name Amen

Sound like today? Someone's doing good and the proud and evil one's plan is to do harm. They did with Jesus, and it didn't work. Oh, it looked bad the whole time...but then, God turned it all around. Being His children, God is going to do the same in this time for our generation. Stand strong and every day, thank God for the good we cannot see yet. Hallelujah! Glory to God!

THREE HUNDRED FIFTEEN

Proverbs 15:1

A soft answer turns away wrath, but a harsh word stirs up anger.

In Jesus name Amen

To give someone a piece of your mind is not in the BIBLE.

THREE HUNDRED SIXTEEN

John 15:5

I am the vine; you are the branches. Whoever abides in me and I in him, he it is that bears much fruit, for apart from me you can do nothing.

In Jesus name Amen

It's a two-way street. Your part is to continue to stay with the Lord and His ways. God's part is to give you everything pertaining to life. No missing parts.

THREE HUNDRED SEVENTEEN

Colossians 2:15

He disarmed the rulers and authorities and put them to open shame, by triumphing over them in him.

In Jesus name Amen

Jesus disarmed Satan and all his workers. So don't let this shameless, naked, no power, no authority holder rule over you any longer!!! You are the one Jesus did this for and He gave you the AUTHORITY, the full Armor with confidence to command all things under your feet!!! Faith comes from hearing the Word of God. If you have trouble believing God and His Word, then my friend take wisdom and get yourself to church because like never before, you are going to need Faith in His Word to take control of your world!!!

THREE HUNDRED EIGHTEEN

Job 42:10

And the Lord restored the fortunes of Job, when he had prayed for his friends. And the Lord gave Job twice as much as he had before.

In Jesus name Amen.

Don't throw everything out just because it's in the Old Testament!! Learn from the History of our sisters and brothers, from the time that has passed. When you're in need, you pray for others. The same people who were telling Job to curse God and die, are the very people he prayed for. A lesson worth learning. It's God's way that makes our life great, just do it by the Book. (The Bible.)

THREE HUNDRED NINETEEN

Exodus 10:23

They did not see one another, nor did anyone rise from his place for three days, but all the people of Israel had light where they lived.

In Jesus name Amen

Always focus on what you have and not what you don't have. God's Children will always have favor.

THREE HUNDRED TWENTY

Proverbs 3:5-6

Trust in the Lord with all your heart, and do not lean on your own understanding.
In all your ways acknowledge him, and he will make straight your paths.

In Jesus name Amen

Are you feeling a little bit unsure?

Follow and apply God's Word a lot more.

TRUST in GOD = FAITH in GOD = GREAT EXPERIENCE with GOD.

THREE HUNDRED TWENTY-ONE

Matthew 24:44

For this reason, you also must be ready; for the Son of Man is coming at an hour when you do not think He will.

In Jesus name Amen

Death will come. We are never ready for physical death, but we know it will happen. It's so important to be ready for Spiritual Life with Jesus for infinity. Please don't wait another minute to ask God to come into your heart. God wants you just the way you are right now. The most important decision in your life for Earth and for Heaven.

THREE HUNDRED TWENTY-TWO

John 3:16

For God so loved the world, that He gave His only begotten Son, that whoever believes in Him shall not perish, but have eternal life.

In Jesus name Amen

If you already know this, are you sharing it with those who don't know? Take their forever life out of Hell and walk them into living forever in Heaven. Oh my!!! Tell them the good news!!

THREE HUNDRED TWENTY-THREE

Luke 17:14

When He saw them, He said to them, "Go and show yourselves to the priests." And as they were going, they were cleansed.

In Jesus name Amen

Jesus never touched them to heal them. He spoke Words! Jesus said, "GO." (Action on their part.) By THEIR faith they went believing! As they went, they were HEALED! You are already Healed, and Healing comes in different ways for different people. Sometimes it is a complete Miracle from the Lord. And sometimes they come when: you have heard the Word of God, when you walk by Faith, allowing time for manifestation is another way, and by someone touching you is another. Healed/Healings come in many ways and forms. Healed/Healings is already here! Speak out the words, "I am HEALED" and activate your faith with your voice! You must believe it. Satan will yell back "No, you are not healed, stupid!!" You don't have to yell; you can whisper and laugh in Satan's face while you say: "I am healed." in Jesus' name!!!! Now accept your HEALED body and GO. Hallelujah to the Lamb of God!!

THREE HUNDRED TWENTY-FOUR

Matthew 11:28-30

Come to me, all you who are weary and burdened, and I will give you rest.
Take my yoke upon you and learn from me, for I am gentle and humble in heart, and you will find rest for your souls.
For my yoke is easy and my burden is light."

In Jesus name Amen

Just come as you are and know God is gentle and humble. Get to know Him in a deeper way. Find time every day with just you and God and leave the world outside. God is love.

THREE HUNDRED TWENTY-FIVE

Matthew 7:7

Ask, and it will be given to you; seek, and you will find; knock, and it will be opened to you.

In Jesus name Amen

Are you asking?

Are you knocking?

Are you seeking?

God said, it will be given. God said, you find. God said, it will be open. Yes, and Amen!!!

THREE HUNDRED TWENTY-SIX

Matthew 13:41-42

The Son of Man will send out his angels, and they will weed out of his kingdom everything that causes sin and all who do evil.
They will throw them into the blazing furnace, where there will be weeping and gnashing of teeth.

In Jesus name Amen

Rest assured that ALL EVIL, even those who are seated in high office in our USA, working against our almighty God that CAUSES SIN and DO EVIL who think they are above our Lord Jesus Christ will be weeded out. They will see the blazing furnace. (Infinity) Keep praying for them. Jesus did give His life for them like He did for us. We did do evil against God and even committed sin, but someone was praying for us, and we are saved and changed. God doesn't want His creation to end up in Hell. No, not even one, but by choice, they can. Prayer does work if we would truly pray for them! Let's do things God's Way and pray for our enemies and let God judge on their final day.

THREE HUNDRED TWENTY-SEVEN

Luke 4:8

And Jesus answered and said unto him, get thee behind me, Satan: for it is written, Thou shalt worship the Lord thy God, and him only shalt thou serve.

In Jesus name Amen

What do you have that you would hesitate to give away if the Lord asked you? That's something to think about and ask yourself why would you hesitate? It's not for you to tell me but just realize things you may worship and not realize it. If God asks you to give away anything, know He has a blessing ready for you because of your obedience.

THREE HUNDRED TWENTY-EIGHT

Hebrews 13:8

Jesus Christ is the same yesterday and today and forever.

In Jesus name Amen

Jesus is the Truth! When standing on God's Word which never changes, you can change facts into truth! Once you get this in your heart, you are the overcomer! Like Jesus said, He calls YOU overcomer!!!

THREE HUNDRED TWENTY-NINE

Proverb 9:8-9

Do not rebuke mockers or they will hate you; rebuke the wise and they will love you. Instruct the wise and they will be wiser still; teach the righteous and they will add to their learning.

In Jesus name Amen

Which are you?
Mocker/scoffer?
Wise person?
Not sure?

Read again and see how you take someone's instructions or correction. Be honest and be who Jesus made YOU to be.

THREE HUNDRED THIRTY

2 Corinthians 9:8

And God is able to make all grace abound to you, so that always having all sufficiency in everything, you may have an abundance for every good deed;

In Jesus name Amen

Sufficiency: means to meet one's needs. God has said He is able to meet all your needs in everything!! Now go dig into God's Word and find out what verse you need to stand on until you have all sufficiently in the area that you are lacking. Stop living below God's Way as the world does. Start living up to God's way as He planned for you, it is your choice. Nothing is impossible for God!! In Emotion... in trust... in Fear... in financing... in pain... in all things! Be patient and keep your faith. Contact me and I will pray for you and help you find that verse you're digging for to stand on!! Know God is right there where you are, just call out to him! God is real and so is His Word.

THREE HUNDRED THIRTY-ONE

2 Corinthians 5:17

Therefore, if anyone is in Christ, he is a new creation. The old has passed away; behold, the new has come.

In Jesus name Amen

Behold, YOU are new and the old you has passed away. For you to grow, you must feed your physical body with physical food. In the Spiritual world, you must feed your spirit man with spiritual food to grow. Oh, what a table the Lord has set before you. Come enjoy the Spiritual food the Lord has for you!!! No charge! Jesus Christ has paid the price for you to come and eat from His table freely.

THREE HUNDRED THIRTY-TWO

John 14:6

Jesus said to him, "I am the way, and the truth, and the life. No one comes to the Father, except through me.

In Jesus name Amen

Any other way to God is nothing but a thief! Don't follow them!!!!

THREE HUNDRED THIRTY-THREE

1 Corinthians 15:33

Do not be misled: "Bad company corrupts good character."

In Jesus name Amen

If you find yourself saying, it doesn't bother me, you are being deceived! In your soul, you are tormenting your right standing with God. Don't play with Satan and then complain to God that Satan has a dark cloud over your life. You cannot have two God's!!! DON'T BE DECEIVED! God said, BAD COMPANY corrupts good character so don't hang with them, instead... pray for them.

THREE HUNDRED THIRTY-FOUR

MATTHEW 24:12

And because iniquity shall abound, the love of many shall wax cold.

In Jesus name Amen

Have you seen how a candle is made? You take a wick and dip it repeatedly, ever so slowly into hot wax and before long it becomes heavy and thick. That's how you become "waxed." You take your Christian life and let yourself be dipped into the worlds thinking and its ways over and over again. Next thing you notice, you are heavy and now your love is wax cold for the Lord. You think the drinking is ok, you think the cursing is ok, everyone does it! No, your Jesus does not do it and you are His. Walk closer with God and feel that thick hard wax melt off and return to the Love of your life!

THREE HUNDRED THIRTY-FIVE

2 Timothy 3:15-17

You have known the Holy Scriptures since you were a child. These Scriptures are able to make you wise. And that wisdom leads to salvation through faith in Christ Jesus.
All Scripture is given by God. And all Scripture is useful for teaching and for showing people what is wrong in their lives. It is useful for correcting faults and teaching the right way to live.
Using the Scriptures, those who serve God will be prepared and will have everything they need to do every good work.

In Jesus name Amen

The Word of God will make you wise and God will always supply everything you need to do His work in your life. That's God's part. Now go and get WISE!!! That's your part.

THREE HUNDRED THIRTY-SIX

Jeremiah 29:11

For I know the plans I have for you, declares the Lord, plans for welfare and not for evil, to give you a future and a hope.

In Jesus name Amen

If Jesus can see the future for YOU. Then trust Him today to see around your corner and over the hill. Let God do the leading and trust Him in every step.

THREE HUNDRED THIRTY-SEVEN

Matthew 5:44

But I tell you, love your enemies and pray for those who persecute you.

In Jesus name Amen

You never know what God has planned for in that prayer for your enemies. Those very same people could be an answer to one of your prayers. Only God can take a bad situation and turn it completely around and leave you blessed.

THREE HUNDRED THIRTY-EIGHT

1 Peter 3:10-12

For "Whoever desires to love life and see good days, let him keep his tongue from evil and his lips from speaking deceit;
let him turn away from evil and do good; let him seek peace and pursue it.
For the eyes of the Lord are on the righteous, and his ears are open to their prayer. But the face of the Lord is against those who do evil."

In Jesus name Amen

Here it is in black and white. Either you want God, or you don't. Just look at your ways and make the decision to keep evil from your tongue.

THREE HUNDRED THIRTY-NINE

2 Kings 5:10

Elisha sent a messenger to say to him, "Go, wash yourself seven times in the Jordan, and your flesh will be restored, and you will be cleansed."

In Jesus name Amen

Yes, you will hear God tell you stuff that sounds crazy, but at the same time you know in your spirit it is the thing to do. Just remember, God loves you and will guide you into good and not bad. Trust and have faith in God and follow Him in everything He guides you to do. After doing what God guides you to do, without knowing the outcome, the outcome is always wonderful. Each step is not easy, but you do become more willing to step out! You are now seeing the love God has for you and the good He has planned for your life. Enjoy your journey with the great I AM!!!

THREE HUNDRED FORTY

Acts 4:30

While you stretch out your hand to heal, and signs and wonders are performed through the name of your holy servant Jesus."

In Jesus name Amen

Whosoever can believe. Are you a whosoever? If you are, step out of the box you put yourself in and get your hands and Faith working!!! Every time I lay hands on anyone, I EXPECT much from my Lord. He has the power and I have the faith, what comes next? Signs and wonders! Give all glory to the Lord! What God says is truth. Let's just do what He says and watch the signs and wonders happen. Faith is NOW!!

THREE HUNDRED FORTY-ONE

Mark 10:15

Truly, I say to you, whoever does not receive the kingdom of God like a child shall not enter it."

In Jesus name Amen

No matter your situation, know your Heavenly Father knows, sees, and will turn things around for you. Walk like a child with trust in God. As a child lives in their parents' house there are house rules to protect you, guide you, to keep you healthy, keep you safe. Go ahead and get excited and jump, dance, sing to your Heavenly Father and see Him dancing with you!!!! He loves you so very much!!!!

THREE HUNDRED FORTY-TWO

1 Timothy 4:1

Now the Spirit expressly says that in later times some will depart from the faith by devoting themselves to deceitful spirits and teachings of demons.

In Jesus name Amen

Check yourself... if you are not following the whole Word of the Lord, then you are no better than the demons themselves! They tell you half of God's Word, then tell you to accept what is politically right and you can stay safe. Men and women of God: check yourselves and don't be misled in the smallest lie! Later times are happening right now! If you are not standing for God, then you are handing over your very own life to the deceitful spirit and demons. They are laughing behind your back because they want you to burn in Hell with them! You may not believe in Hell, but the demons know it's real, that's why they're fighting for you! When you die, your spirit walks out of the physical body and your spirit lives in Hell or Heaven. Where will you spend eternity?

THREE HUNDRED FORTY-THREE

Hebrews 10:25

Not giving up meeting together, as some are in the habit of doing, but encouraging one another--and all the more as you see the Day approaching."

In Jesus name Amen

Wow!! Look at this verse. God knew in later days, some of us would fall in a habit not to meet up in church because of the virus. Here we are, a few years after the pandemic and able to meet up again and a lot of Christians have decided to stay home and just watch from their cell phones or computers. It's amazing how we make a way to get to our jobs no matter what yet, we are missing church. The doors are open now, let's worship our Jesus Christ together in church where we can get encouragement and stand strong. Unity of the church can get through anything together. The days are approaching of dark days, dark hours, and dark ways. We need Jesus Christ, and we need each other. Come and let's assemble and grow stronger. We are going to need this strength in the days ahead.

THREE HUNDRED FORTY-FOUR

Matthew 14:31-33

Immediately Jesus stretched out His hand and took hold of him, and said to him, "You of little faith, why did you doubt?"
When they got into the boat, the wind stopped.
And those who were in the boat worshiped Him, saying, "You are certainly God's Son!"

In Jesus name Amen

Who is in your boat with you? You will have storms and different situations come but with the Lord in your life your storms and these situations will turn to bless you. When the water comes, you will float! When the wind blows, you will go higher! In any situation, you will win. Don't believe it? Then it will not happen for you. Now for those who choose to live with Jesus in your boat, it will happen! Get excited!!!!

THREE HUNDRED FORTY-FIVE

Romans 5:8

But God demonstrates His own love for us in this: while we were still sinners, Christ died for us.

In Jesus name Amen

You are worth Jesus's death. You have not shocked God one little bit by your wrong choices. God decided! Even while you decide to do what you want, when you want and how you want! Even when you curse His Holy Name, He wants YOU! Come as you are unto Jesus. Yes, just as you are! Christ died for YOU! You don't have to understand His love and you don't have to wait until you're perfect. Come as you are! Yep, drugs, alcohol and all the above. God is a gentleman; he is waiting for you. You can count on God not to turn His back on you like so called friends. Just come!! Never put off tomorrow what you can do today! Jesus is here NOW!!!

THREE HUNDRED FORTY-SIX

2 Chronicles 7:14

If my people, which are called by my name, shall humble themselves, and pray, and seek my face, and turn from their wicked ways; then will I hear from heaven, and will forgive their sin, and will heal their land.

In Jesus name Amen

If you think God is in control, you better think and read this again!! If Christians (His people) who pray, seek, and turn from our own way (us Christians) God will forgive us and heal our land!!! Does our Christian land USA look healed??? God is telling us when we turn things around by praying and turn from our wicked ways, then this is when HE moves. Christians: stop playing with religion and get a relationship with God. PRAY and stop agreeing with this world to stay politically correct! Agree with God and then PRAY!

THREE HUNDRED FORTY-SEVEN

James 5:12

But above all, my brothers, do not swear, either by heaven or by earth or by any other oath, but let your "yes" be yes and your "no" be no, so that you may not fall under condemnation.

In Jesus name Amen

Smile and with a simple word of "yes" or "no," be on your way. God's Ways are really very easy.

THREE HUNDRED FORTY-EIGHT

Titus 3:5

He saved us, not on the basis of deeds which we have done in righteousness, but according to His mercy, by the washing of regeneration and renewing by the Holy Spirit.

In Jesus name Amen

Come to God in Jesus Name and ask Him to be Lord of your life. It is not based on earning your way to Heaven! It's believing Jesus Christ is the son of God and YOU invite Him into your life. Rich or poor! Smart or not! Big or small! Country or city! Just come and ask God, in Jesus' name in your life and in your heart. Do this and I will see you in Heaven with your family. Thank you, Lord!

THREE HUNDRED FORTY-NINE

Jeremiah 29:13

You will seek me and find me, when you seek
me with all your heart.

In Jesus name Amen

Your heart will lead you to the Lord. Seek God
with all your heart. Be prepared for action when
you seek, because He will guide you into truth
for you to move forward.

THREE HUNDRED FIFTY

1 Corinthians 2:16

For who has known the mind of the Lord, that he will instruct Him? But we have the mind of Christ.

In Jesus name Amen

It's not your physical mind that has the mind of Christ but your born-again spirit man inside you!!! Now you can know inside you, you do have the mind of Christ! That's why Satan hates you so much because you become more aware of the power you have inside you which makes him powerless!!!! Get excited! It is the new you, the born-again child!!!!

THREE HUNDRED FIFTY-ONE

Mark 11:25

But when you are praying, first forgive anyone you are holding a grudge against, so that your Father in heaven will forgive your sins, too."

In Jesus name Amen

God is telling you: you could forgive but you choose not to. Go ahead and find that love you have inside your heart and forgive that person. It's not because that person deserves your forgiveness, but you deserve the FREEDOM you get for giving that forgiveness. God has made this a gift for you and because of Jesus, you deserve this gift.

THREE HUNDRED FIFTY-TWO

Revelation 3:21

To him that overcometh will I grant to sit with me in my throne, even as I also overcame, and am set down with my Father in his throne.

In Jesus name Amen

Be the overcomer in every area of your life.

Finance = Giving tithe and offering.

Healing = Words you use every day.

Love = Kindness and caring.

Faith = Walking with God no matter what!

Peace = Joy.

Be an overcomer with the armor of God every day and you will sit with the Lord! Best news I have ever heard! It's worth putting down your ways and picking up God's ways! That's what it's all about! Stop being cute in your own ways and become strong! Get serious, grow up and move forward with the Truth of the Lord and then live it. You will have more fun than you could ever imagine!!!!!

THREE HUNDRED FIFTY-THREE

1 Peter 1:15-16

But as he who called you is holy, you also be
holy in all your conduct,
since it is written, "You shall be holy, for I am
holy."

In Jesus name Amen

Help me Lord be what you have called me to be.
Thank you, God, for guiding me to be more like
you. Today I choose to let my conduct reflect
you, my Lord. You call me your child. Thank
you for your Grace and Mercy. I will get to know
you more and learn your ways. And when I fall
sometimes, I know with your right hand you
will pick me up to walk again. Like a wonderful
Father, you will do it with love. Thank you, my
Holy Father.

THREE HUNDRED FIFTY-FOUR

Hebrews 10:23

Let us hold fast the confession of our hope without wavering, for he who promised is faithful.

In Jesus name Amen

What Word of the Lord are you reading everyday so you will not lose your hope, so you will not waver? You NEED to know God's Word to know what He has promised for your situation. Remember God is faithful to His Word, not sometimes but All THE TIME!!!

THREE HUNDRED FIFTY-FIVE

Mark 16:15

He said to them, "Go into all the world and preach the gospel to all creation."

In Jesus name Amen

You say, "I have no idea how to share the Word of God with someone." Start with Y.O.U. You are a someone. Open the Bible and find a verse to read out loud and proud! Get to know the living Word of God. Just one verse at a time or a chapter. First stir your own self up! Then just like the wind blowing on an open fire, it gets bigger and burns hotter. So will your heart for the Lord and next thing you know, you are telling someone in a small conversation how Great He is! You do this and I will do this and then they will do this, and we will be able to reach the world. YOU got this!

THREE HUNDRED FIFTY-SIX

John 10:16

I have other sheep that are not of this sheep pen. I must bring them also. They too will listen to my voice, and there shall be one flock and one shepherd.

In Jesus name Amen

This should make you excited. Way back then, Jesus was talking about you and I. Jews and now the Gentiles (us). Did you notice Jesus never said black, white, Spanish, or Asian? With God, it's two: the Jews and the Gentiles! We all belong to Him, and He is calling you to be His children. Satan divides us to separate us from God to keep us weak and fighting each other. God calls us together to make us strong and love each other as one big born-again family. Time for us to unite and let Jesus be our true Shepherd. Listen for His voice because He is talking to His sheep, not the world. Get back to doing it by the book as a family. Oh, how He loves you!

THREE HUNDRED FIFTY-SEVEN

Acts 1:8

But you will receive power when the Holy Spirit has come upon you; and you shall be My witnesses both in Jerusalem, and in all Judea and Samaria, and even to the remotest part of the earth.

In Jesus name Amen

We are Jesus's Power of Attorney on Earth. We can't be POA without the power! Yep, here it is!! If you don't believe, you don't have to give it another thought, it won't work for you anyway. But, if you believe, just keep reading and soon it will be like a seed that is planted in your heart and takes root. By having Faith in God, you now step out in what God has said. Watch the power in the name of Jesus turn things around on this earth because you have believed. Born again child, God always keeps His Word!

THREE HUNDRED FIFTY-EIGHT

Revelation 21:8

But as for the cowardly, the faithless, the detestable, as for murderers, the sexually immoral, sorcerers, idolaters, and all liars, their portion will be in the lake that burns with fire and sulfur, which is the second death."

In Jesus name Amen

God will not surprise you at the end of life with Hell. Here, He tells you clearly if you walk away from Him and live your life against His Word you have put yourself in Hell, not Him. It's not that God turns His back on you, you have turned your back on Him. God knows when you are doing your best for Him. He also knows when you are just having a "could care less about it attitude!" Get to know your God, spend time in His Word and read the truth for yourself. Guess work is not knowledge.

THREE HUNDRED FIFTY-NINE

Malachi 3:10

Bring the full tithe into the storehouse, that there may be food in my house. And thereby put me to the test, says the Lord of hosts, if I will not open the windows of heaven for you and pour down for you a blessing until there is no more need.

In Jesus name Amen

If you think this is all about money, think again. God said it, not your Pastor. If your Pastor is preaching all of God's Word, he better be preaching about tithes and offerings. This is about YOU being obedient to God, not man! You do as God says and if someone is misusing the money, that is between them and God! You obey! You give! It's about you being obedient to the Lord. This is the only place in God's Word where he says: "TRY ME!" Go ahead and be obedient and blessings will run you down. This is not about you and a Pastor, or about you deciding what they need to do with the money you give. If you are truly giving it to the Lord, once it leaves your hand, now it's between God and the Pastor. If a Preacher is living what he is preaching, God is blessing him because he is being obedient!! I look to see if the Pastor is living a prosperous life and teaching the bible. If he is, then I am all in. Don't let Satan take you down the road from the past Pastors. God is dealing with them! Satan wants you to think: "it's all about the money!" NOT! It's about obedience and trusting God. Satan knows if you get this, there is NO stopping your blessings. It's not about the money at all. It's about your love and obedience to the one you say you love. If you open the door, God will open a window to blessings that will overflow in YOUR life. God is a sure thing!! Go ahead and try Him!

THREE HUNDRED SIXTY

Proverbs 12:25

Anxiety in a mans heart weighs him down, but a good word makes him glad.

In Jesus name Amen

Exchange your anxiety for a good Word. The Bible has many "GOOD WORDS!"

Now believe, trust, and have faith in what you read. Shout out loud about what you have found from the book of the Lord Jesus Christ.

THREE HUNDRED SIXTY-ONE

Romans 1:21

For although they knew God, they neither glorified Him as God nor gave thanks to Him, but their thinking became futile and their foolish hearts were darkened.

In Jesus name Amen

1. Glorified

2. Thanks

In EVERYTHING, give glory to God and thanks to God. We can snuggle up to the Lord and give Him all our heart. Give ALL GLORY and THANKS to our Lord. He is a Great and Awesome God! Let's never forget what He has done for us on the cross. Oh, how He loves you!

THREE HUNDRED SIXTY-TWO

Psalms 126:6

He who goes out weeping, bearing the seed for sowing, shall come home with shouts of joy, bringing his sheaves with him.

In Jesus name Amen

Plant a seed for Jesus in people's hearts. Do it in love and always in God's truth. If you don't plant a seed for Jesus, what will you get back? Nothing! Go ahead and plant that seed in someone's heart of that love Jesus has for them! In due time, you will see the change! You will shout with joy!!

I see family members and friends following Jesus and because of that seed, they are born again today. I shout out every day! Let's help as many as we can to know that sweet love Jesus Christ has for them. That means you have to get out of that box of shame, shyness, timidness, and whatever else is holding you back from doing your part for the Kingdom of God.

BE BOLD IN CHRIST!!

THREE HUNDRED SIXTY-THREE

Proverbs 4:10

Hear, my son, and accept my words, that the years of your life may be many.

In Jesus name Amen

The Lord never said to understand His Words. God said, "accept my Words." That means even when you don't understand, you still accept His Word and apply it to your life. Abraham did not understand why the Lord asked him to sacrifice his son, he simply accepted the Lord's Word and applied that Word to his life that day. Abraham stepped out in faith and trusted his God. He was obedient in what he was told to do. His life was blessed, and he had years added unto him.

Read, accept, and apply your faith. Your life will be blessed, and your years of life will be added to you. Remember when you don't understand His Word, go ahead and trust and apply His Word to your life. Wonderful things will happen! Why are some people blessed so much? Watch and see! You will find they really applied and accepted the Word of God.

Why would God give you a Word that would destroy you? The one who calls you SON. Not happening today or any other day! Trust the one who loves you more than your physical mind can comprehend. Go ahead and start today! Do it HIS way!!

THREE HUNDRED SIXTY-FOUR

Proverbs 16:3

Commit your actions to the Lord, and your plans will succeed.

In Jesus name Amen

When you line up your life, your ways, your plans, and you commit to the Lord, you will always succeed! It's about His timing and His order. All Hell will run and hide! It's all worth doing His way and receiving a blessing you cannot contain. Hallelujah! Hallelujah! Hallelujah!

Go ahead... tithe, have conversations with Him, apply His Word no matter how often you have to bite your lip, take your position and take your authority!

THREE HUNDRED SIXTY-FIVE

Jeremiah 33:3

Call to me and I will answer you, and will tell you great and hidden things that you have not known.

In Jesus name Amen

If you are in the Kingdom of God, you are a child of God and can ask questions and get answers. So, when you go to bed, ask your question to The Almighty God, King of Kings. Go to sleep knowing He hears you and thank Him for your answer in the morning. Trust your God! Yes, He truly is a wonderful, awesome God! Life with God is the coolest way of Life!

Our God is:

Jehovah Elohim – Strong Creator

Jehovah Elyon – Lord, most high

Jehovah Adonai – Lord, my master

Jehovah Nissi – Lord, my banner

Jehovah Rapha – Lord, my healer

Jehovah Elolam – Everlasting God

Jehovah Elroi – God who sees

Jehovah Sabboth – Lord of Host

Jehovah Rohi – Lord, my shepherd

Jehovah Tsideknu – Lord, our righteous

Jehovah Shalom – Lord our peace

Jehovah Chereb – Lord our Sword

Jehovah Elkanna – Jealous God

Jehovah Ezer – Lord, my help

Jehovah Avinu – Lord, our Father

Jehovah Hashopet – Lord, our Judge

Jehovah Ori - Lord, my light

Jehovah Elgibbor - Mighty God

Jehovah Immeka - Lord is with you

Jehovah Elnose - God that forgave

Jehovah Jireh - Lord, my provider

ACKNOWLEGDEMENTS

I want to thank my church family for giving of their time and talent for God's work, here on Earth, towards this book.

Stacey Rose, for being my ghost writer. Stacey's favorite verse is Colossians 1: 13-14, For he has rescued us from the dominion of darkness and brought us into the kingdom of the Son he loves, in whom we have redemption, the forgiveness of sins.

Philip Meredith is the artist of the beautiful picture in this book. Philip's favorite verse is Titus 2: 13-14, while we wait for the blessed hope—the appearing of the glory of our great God and Savior, Jesus Christ, [14]who gave himself for us to redeem us from all wickedness and to purify for himself a people that are his very own, eager to do what is good.

Becky Hallock, for editing this book. Becky's favorite verse is 2 Timothy 1:7, For God hath not given us the spirit of fear; but of power, and of love, and of a sound mind.

Lutricia Lopez, she is my backbone. When God told me to write this book, she was the angel who had sent the text that asked if I had ever thought about placing my devotionals in a book. She prayed and held my hand through it all. Lutricia's favorite verse is 3 John 1:2, Beloved, I wish above all things that thou mayest prosper and be in health, even as thy soul prospereth.

Denise Ryman, God gave me a full-grown daughter. She needed a momma, and I needed a daughter. With her high spirit and boldness, we fit together like a glove. She is my daughter without a doubt. I will never let go of you! During this time while writing this book, she was my right hand and my left hand behind the scenes. What a blessing God sent me when He sent you. You are truly mine. Denise's favorite scripture is Romans 8:38-39 For I am persuaded, that neither death, nor life, nor angels, nor principalities, nor powers, nor things

Jim Cox, he has been a long-time friend of mine. Even if we don't see each other or talk often, Jim is always there for me. Jim did the final editing on my book. Jim's favorite scripture is Jeremiah 29:11, For I know the thoughts that I think towards you, saith the Lord, thoughts of peace, and not of evil, to give you an expected end.

My son, Charles Johnson, was sent to me from God. God used my son in so many ways in all my situations in life. Charles is my heartbeat. When things would get tough, he would say, "Mom? What does God say?" Then his next words would be, "Yes you can!" His soft smile, sweet spirit, his kindness towards everyone, teaches me that the walk is narrow, but "I can do this!" My son's favorite verse is Joshua 1:9 Have I not commanded you? Be strong and courageous. Do not be afraid; do not be discouraged, the Lord your God will be with you wherever you go.

No Tears

Wipe your tears,
Wipe them dry;
Do not cry because I died.

I fly like an eagle,
Up high above the sky,
My spirit feels light,
I know this is right.

~ 430 ~

I see the Glory of God,
I tell you I am alive.
I am just in a different body,
And God is right by my side.

I am so happy to have no more pain.
I am in a world which is hard to explain.

I am home and not alone.
There is love and peace
Which has been given to me.
I am alive and alright.

Wipe your tears.
Wipe them dry;
Because I am alive?

~Penny Beavers

In Memory of Lawerence Robert Plaster
August 27, 1994

Made in the USA
Middletown, DE
15 December 2023

45886101R00239